DECEPTION

BE NOT DECEIVED

by

Retired Officer Ronald L. Waldron

authorHOUSE®

AuthorHouse™
1663 Liberty Drive, Suite 200
Bloomington, IN 47403
www.authorhouse.com
Phone: 1-800-839-8640

First published by AuthorHouse 6/27/2008

ISBN: 978-1-4343-9753-9 (sc)

Printed in the United States of America
Bloomington, Indiana

This book is printed on acid-free paper.

DISCOVER THE DECEPTIONS:

You can not fool all the people all the time.

Be not deceived, God is not mocked, for what so ever a man soweth, that shall he also reap.

The terror attacks of September 11, 2001 are increasingly used to justify systematic surveillance and the dismantling of constitutional rights. Even European countries have helped to establish Guantanomo-like secret prisons, where torture in all probability takes place.

Iraq was attacked based on falsified evidence causing the death of hundreds of thousands of people, widespread destruction, destabilization and contamination with cancer-causing depleted uranium munitions.

Now plans to attack Iran, and the possibility of a new World War have been made public, meeting resistance even from moderate elements within the military due to the unforeseeable consequences.

Faced with the choice between a war, which according to some western leaders, will last for many years or a possible peaceful transformation we support the following:

1) Impeach: Waging wars of aggression contrary to international law and committing crimes against humanity.

2) International investigation of the September 11, 2001 terror attacks. They are used as the central justification for the "War on Terror", but well documented evidence shows that the official

explanation of 9/11 cannot be correct. International personalities in science, politics, and culture, including high-ranking military veterans, have called for a new investigation.

3) Immediate military withdrawal from Afghanistan and Iraq, and no attack against Iran. International prohibition of war as a means of conflict resolution. Military intervention and export of weapons should be criminalized. In a civilized society torture must be prohibited in any form.

4) Conversion of military industries to civilian purposes and the development of ecological and sustainable energy resources. According to the UN environmental agency, a fraction of the annual global defense expenditure could ensure that all humans have access to clean water and a basic supply of food and healthcare.

This statement is based on a commitment to non-violence and tolerance of all ethnic groups and religions. Two devastating World Wars and historical catastrophes like the Nazi Holocaust must always remind us of the worst consequences of nationalism, racism and incitement to war.

Candidates for public office, high and low, are bewitched -frightened is the more accurate word - by an unwarranted but costly fear of the foreign lobby that functions on behalf of the State of Israel.

Comb through the millions of words expressed by the "final three" in the presidential sweepstakes - Barack Obama, Hillary Rodham Clinton and John McCain - and you will not find a word, not even a syllable, of criticism of the longstanding US policy bias that heavily favors Israel, a policy that imposes a staggering burden on US society and infuriates Muslims worldwide, including eight million who are US citizens.

A search of major media -print, radio and television - has virtually the same result: silence. The internet is one of the few places where one can find thoughtful and candid examinations of Israel's dominance of US society.

This silence is a phenomenon unknown elsewhere in the world. Discussion of the US bias and its terrible consequences are common in periodicals in Britain, France, Germany, all Arab countries, and most other nations, even in Israel, whose Hebrew newspapers and journals regularly discuss candidly and deeply the bad behavior of Israel's government.

US citizens seldom see reminders that Israel, with US encouragement, came into being in 1948 by the sword and has expanded its domain and carried out its destruction and humiliation of Palestinian society the same way ever since. The bias in media coverage leads uninformed people to view Israelis, not Palestinians, as the victims. Such was part of the 2006 mandate by the people, that to present has been ignored, but The World against the human rights violations is yet to be dealt with. It has been David against Goliath, but the end result will be the same as Bible history about suppression.

Grants to Israel have cost US taxpayers over $1.2 trillion. That sum includes, as it should, the cost of servicing the annual outlays as new debt.

In 1982, Israel, using US-donated arms, killed over 17,000 people in the environs of Beirut, Lebanon. In addition to the death toll, according to data compiled by journalist Alison Weir surgeons amputated over 1,000 limbs in the aftermath of just one day's assault. Two years ago, Israeli forces killed over 1,000 people in another invasion of Lebanon. Most of the dead in both invasions were civilians.

- Israel now keeps 1.5 million Palestinians imprisoned in the desolate Gaza Strip, because, in a well-monitored election, they voted into power Hamas, an organization hostile to Israel's conquests. Another two million are cordoned off like cattle behind 20-foot walls and fences in the West Bank.

- In recent years, Israelis have destroyed over 10,000 Palestinian homes in East Jerusalem and elsewhere in occupied Palestine.

The invasions of Lebanon, the mistreatment of Palestinians, and the destruction of homes are crimes under international law. None of this would have happened if any US president in the last 30 years had the courage to refuse to finance Israel's conquests. If the US government had suspended financial, military, and political support Israel could not have carried out these monstrous crimes.

None of the three candidates seriously contending for the presidency says a word about suspending aid until Israel stops its criminal acts. Not even the slightest hint. Indeed, each mentions Israel only with peons of praise and pledges of unqualified support. Why? Fear, that is why.

Is the US fated to have another president take office next January who is afraid to challenge the lobby for a small scofflaw country the size of New Jersey? Obama is the only one not accepting their money, and will work for the will of the people.

WHO REALLY DID IT?

JFK, MLK, RFK, & 911:
MOSSAD CAN NOT BE ILLEMATED FROM ANY CASE!!

Lucky Larry wants $12.3 billion more for 9/11 By Jerry Mazza 03 Apr 2008 like the proverbial bad penny, Lucky Larry Silverstein keeps popping up. He's back and he's bad again. Not content with the nearly $4.6 billion in insurance payments he received to cover his losses at the World Trade Center, he is now seeking $12.3 billion in damages from the airlines and airport security companies for the 9/11 attack in a suit filed in 2004.

A statement by Larry Silverstein indicates World Trade Center 7 was demolished, and all evidence shows this occurred. Why was WTC 7 rigged for demolition?

Meanwhile, Flight 93 had to be shot down. Its nose was found eight miles from the tail in a Pennsylvania field. Such stories were made up to explain the mess! The terrorists let the toughest guys get together to use their personal handsets to call home. Someone heard, "Let's get rolling, boys." They rushed the cockpit and saved the nation.

Except, cell phones don't work from 35,000 feet up. http://physics911.ca/org/modules/weblog/details.php?blog_id=65

CeeCee Lyles husband said that he saw the caller ID, Ed Felt had called from a bathroom, and Air phone cords don't reach that far.

As a matter of fact, in a bathroom, one would expect that it would be harder to make a call, probably bringing down the power about in 1/2 (3dB).

Ted Olson first said that Barbara had used a cell phone, and then he said she was in the bathroom, then he said she forgot her purse and had to borrow a credit card from someone to make an air phone call. His story kept changing.

If you look at the flight maps, most of the calls for flight 93 "should" have been made at 35,000ft or even above. http://team8plus.org/e107_plugins/forum/forum_viewtopic.php?315

And who were the select passengers on board? Pretty unusual and tiny group, no?

Flight 93 had only forty four people in total, including four suspected hijackers. Thirty seven passengers (excluding crew) on a plane that holds around two hundred people http://team8plus.org/content.php?article.8 23 of those (at least) bought tickets at the last minute!

Also several people came from flight 91 that was cancelled.

Did ANYONE buy tickets for flight 93 ahead of time???

QUESTIONS FOR LARRY

In 1980 Larry Silverstein won a bid to buy the last undeveloped parcel from the Port Authority of New York.

The Port Authority is not a municipal property. It was founded by and owned by the Rockefeller family.

When the attacks occurred, Larry Silverstein was at home debating with his wife about plans to move his headquarters to the 88th floor of the North Tower. His son Roger was at 7 World Trade Center but was not hurt.

This, of course, was a lie. He was not debating his wife and his son was out of danger.

How concerned should we be therefore that Larry Silverstein Properties bought the lease from MetLife for Chicago's Sears Tower in March 2004?

We should be extremely concerned.

Following the attacks, Larry Silverstein was awarded an insurance payment of more than three and a half billion dollars to settle his seven-week-old insurance policy [3]. In addition, the Larry Silverstein group sued the insurers liable for the World Trade Center for another three and a half billion dollars, claiming that by an obscure clause in their contract, the two planes constituted two separate terrorist attacks [4]. In total, Larry Silverstein was awarded nearly $7.2 billion in insurance money following the destruction of the Twin Towers [5].

No point losing, now is there?

We now get to Larry's politics. What do we discover? His first customer for the new Building 7 is a Chinese revolutionary. Larry may have owned the WTC inside, but the outside concourse was Israeli. And who did Larry support in the last Israeli election but the king of chopping Israel to nothing, the great, now-headless, Ariel Sharon.

http://www.nytimes.com/2006/04/13/nyregion/13wtc.html?_r=1 &n=Top%2fReference%2fTimes%20Topics%2fPeople%2fS%2fL arry Silverstein%2c%20Larry%20A%2e&oref=slogin

He is, by most accounts, an unusual businessman, especially in China. He stresses vision and serving his country as much as the bottom line. He said his real interests were history, Marx, Hegel and Mao.

Then there are the pictures of Che Guevara and Yasser Arafat in his office. He explained that they were both revolutionaries, emphasizing that he admired Mr. Arafat's discipline and courage, not his politics.

"He spent his whole life trying to achieve one thing," Mr. Feng said. "He had great determination; real perseverance."

*

On September 12, 2001, The Jerusalem Post reported: "Frank Lowy, who emigrated to Australia from Israel in 1952, owns the 99-year lease for the 425,000 square foot retail portion of the destroyed World Trade Center...Westfield said today that it has insurance cover against terrorist attacks and its earnings will not be materially affected."

http://www.israelnationalnews.com/news.php3?id=90159

A report by Israel's Channel Ten television reporter Raviv Drucker last night provided a detailed report on the Sunday night affair. He related how the organizer and hostess - NIna Rosenwald - sent letters to selected invitees asking for $10,000 per person or couple, and how the 5th Avenue location was closed off for over an hour for what the police described as a "top secret" reason. Only the 15 invited couples were permitted to enter Rosenwald's apartment, after having paid the minimum amount in advance.

Rosenwald is a member of the CFR (Council of Foreign Relations).

Among the participants at the dinner were World Trade Center insurance beneficiary Larry Silverstein.

A reporter asked Larry Silverstein on his way out if Sharon had thanked him for his donation. Larry Silverstein replied, "No. But it's not necessary; we're here to support the man."

It's simply a God-awful world for Jews and those who know our history is divine. It's even worse because anti-semites can have a field day and not have a clue how dumb they are. Larry Silverstein can call himself as Jew, but he is working for the Sabbataian/ Frankist fold. They hate Judaism and use all their power to make it disappear into the worship of the anti-Jewish fiend, Shabbtai Tzvi.

For, this they created Israel.

But Israel turned religious and that had to be stopped. So the religious began to "disengage." And the more Israel's religious are drawn into the mainstream, the more Iraq, and Afghanistan and Iraq explode.

Even though it's staring the anti-semites in the face, they don't get it. Their closest ally in the Middle East is not the Arabs, who despise them thoroughly, and it is surely not the Israeli peace camp, leading the nation to permanent disengagement and taking the world with it.

It's those right-wing, religious Israeli Jews.
So, by being too dumb to sort it out, the anti-Semites are letting Larry and his New World Order buddies get away with anything they want.

And only one brilliant site on the whole internet figured the whole thing out:
http://www.cloakanddagger.de/media/Grossmann/
Four%20Horsemen/066%20Four%20Riders%20of

NAMES: Leon Fuerth, Andrew Gitlin, Larry Silverstein, Maurice Hank Greenberg, Henry Kissinger, Rahm Emanuel, Ariel Sharon

THEORY: People like Fuerth, Emanuel (U.S. Mossad chief in the Clinton era and White House Rasputin), Kissinger, Gitlin, Greenberg, Larry Silverstein, Sharon are reputedly leaders of a homosexual satanic underground (at least its relatively small Jewish division, overshadowed by its much larger non-Jewish division). They are false Jews. From their midst allegedly came the impulse to assassinate the Israeli Prime Minister and peace dove Yitzhak Rabin, the impulse to provoke the still ongoing Second Intifada in Palestine in fall 2000, and the re-emergence of the known serial murderer and terrorist Ariel Sharon. Sharon was elected Prime Minister of Israel on February 6, 2001 in a special election. This grouping sent several prominent members into the informal committee(s) that perpetrated 9-11 on America. There are multiple links to the second-generation Meyer Lansky crime syndicate. A note of clarification: WE are NOT saying"it was the Jews", and do not quote us as such.

We could have added, from the moment Larry was informed Building 7 HAD to come down because its flight wasn't arriving, to the present day... but I held back. Still, look at the connections. July 11 of last year saw London under attack. And who was there but Rudy Guliani and Binyamin Netanyahu. Were they in town to observe the reaction? Guliani for sure. You needed a mayor to run 9-11. That's why they made him a knight. WE'll say Netanyahu too on gut reaction.

http://www.team8plus.org/e107_plugins/forum/forum_viewtopic.php?387

This report, repeated by IsraelNN.com, added that the Israeli Embassy in London was notified in advance, resulting in Foreign Minister Binyamin Netanyahu remaining in his hotel room rather than make his way to the hotel adjacent to the site of the first explosion, a Liverpool Street train station, where he was to address an economic summit.

The Frankist Michael Chertoff kept New Orleans wet and thirsty for as long as he could, and his cousin kept the 9-11 critics stupid.

http://www.prisonplanet.tv/audio/090305alexresponds.htm

'Who is Benjamin Chertoff, the senior researcher at Popular Mechanics who is behind the article? American Free Press has learned that he is none other than a cousin of Michael Chertoff, the new Secretary of the Department of Homeland Security. This means that Hearst paid Benjamin Chertoff to write an article supporting the seriously flawed explanation that is based on a practically nonexistent investigation of the terror event that directly led to the creation of the massive national security department his cousin now heads.

THIRTY REASONS TO DOUBT
THE OFFICIAL 911 ACCOUNT

TV documentaries to the contrary, a proper analysis of the collapse of each of the World Trade Center towers on 9/11/01 shows that they were not destroyed by the fires and plane impacts.

There are scores of accounts of people hearing and/or seeing explosions before and as the towers fell - including explosions in the lobby or basement of both towers.

Steel girders weighing tens of tons were hurled hundreds of feet and lodged into nearby buildings. Debris in the footprint of each tower was barely two stories high.

The WTC towers fell nearly as fast as the debris that they created, indicating little or no resistance from the floors below.

The Twin Towers each had a massive structural central core. In a gross misrepresentation the 9/11 Commission report referred to this core as "a hollow steel shaft, in which the elevators and stairwells were grouped."

Structural failure in a skyscraper would have an entirely different appearance than that of the collapsing World Trade Center towers. A failing building would be prone to topple, buckle or shed debris instead of being progressively shredded, with perfect radial symmetry, at close to free-fall speed.

The Twin Towers generated vastly more dust and pulverized material than can be accounted for by the total gravitational potential energy of the buildings - the only substantial source of energy available for that destruction.

Mayor Giuliani has stated publicly that he was told the first tower was about to collapse. This is extraordinary considering that in the history of high-rise fires there has never been such a collapse.

The second tower to be hit - the south tower - received less damage than the first yet it collapsed in approximately half the time. Judging by the black smoke, the fire was dying out at the time.

The 5:20 p.m. total collapse of WTC 7, a gleaming 47-story modern skyscraper, has the appearance of a perfectly engineered internal demolition. No plausible explanation has been offered for this and it was ignored by the 9/11 Commission.

The collapse of WTC 7 was reported by the BBC a half hour before it happened, suggesting that the building's destruction was planned and the news scripted.

WTC debris was hastily sold as scrap metal, allowing no proper investigation of the cause of the destruction.

During nearly an hour-and-a-half of national crisis no fighter planes took off from Andrews Air Force Base - a base whose primary assignment is to protect the nation's capital ten miles away.

On the eastern seaboard on 9/11, air defense was deployed from unnecessarily remote bases after unexplainable delays and the planes traveled at a fraction of their top speed - all to arrive too late in both New York and Washington.

There is evidence that five of the "hijackers" had lived at and/or trained at U.S. military bases.

The passenger lists for all four flights, published by the airlines and CNN after September 11th, contained none of the hijackers' names. The flights were only about 30% full.

The documented behavior of the "hijackers" before 9/11 was decidedly un-Muslim.

The FBI's most-wanted list does not mention 9/11 as a crime that Osama bin Laden is sought for. An FBI spokesperson has stated that this was because of no hard evidence.

Numerous pre-9/11 al Qaeda and bin Laden investigations were thwarted or hampered by higher-ups.

President Bush has twice stated in public that before he entered the Emma T. Booker Elementary School classroom he looked at a television and saw the first WTC tower being hit by a plane. Such footage was not shown on TV until later that morning - till after the second crash.

The public has never seen clear pictures or video of the Pentagon being hit. Security camera video from a nearby gas station and a hotel were confiscated by the FBI within a half hour of the attack.

The extreme and roundabout maneuvering of "Flight 77" led to it hitting the only part of the Pentagon that was under construction. Virtually no plane wreckage was visible after the attack.

Plane debris in Pennsylvania was found five mile from the crash site, suggesting that the plane was destroyed while in the air. No plane wreckage was visible at the stated crash site.

A brother and a cousin of the President were affiliated with the security company (Securacom) for the World Trade Center complex.

Calls for an investigation into the attacks were repeatedly brushed aside by the administration. Finally, after 14 months, the 9/11 Commission was formed. The commission ended up being packed with insiders with conflicts of interest and it took as its starting point that al Qaeda was responsible for the attacks.

Max Cleland, the one squeaky wheel on the commission, referred to the limited scope of their work as a "national scandal." President Bush then appointed him to the board of the U.S. Export-

Import Bank and there was no longer a squeaky wheel on the commission.

There were many stock market anomalies just prior to 9/11, indicating individuals with inside knowledge of the planned attacks. The 9/11 Commission has absolved the investors behind these anomalies with comments such as that they could not have had any "conceivable ties to al Qaeda."

There is a large body of material expounding on the aggressive role that the U.S. could or should play on the world stage. This includes frank references to imperial aspirations and to the usefulness of a new Pearl Harbor-type event. The point of view is akin to that of Manifest Destiny.

Plans for wars in Afghanistan and Iraq were set in motion before 9/11/01.

The 9/11 attacks and the threat of terrorism have been invoked repeatedly to gain support for domestic and foreign policy initiatives that otherwise would not be popular. We are told that the new "war on terror" justifies a wholesale shift in our priorities and that that war may not end in our lifetimes.

We saw much this week. Driving in the backwoods of Cyprus looking for bass lakes, We saw the future the British military has built there. We drove by a brand new prison far from the people and as big as a good-sized town.

But nothing was as upsetting as my son and us spending 10 minutes at Israeli passport control, coming and going, and watching the policewomen reading all about us and receiving instructions by phone on what to do about us.

We are now convinced the Israeli authorities are committed to shutting us down. We may help them along a bit. It is clear enough after ten years that not one person anywhere has the courage to fund what we know to save the Jews.

Ronald L. Waldron

And that is a huge mistake because 9-11 may come out and the Jews will be blamed with the Frankist/Sabbataians. More worrisome, they will be disengaged to uselessness while the nation is buried in missiles.

There are so many wonderful options. When will it stop?

GET RID OF THE SPECIAL INTEREST LOBBIES, & THINK TANKS.

FOREIGN LOBBIES PLAYING WITH AMERICAN LIVES, AND TREASURE, GET RID OF THE JERKS!!

AEI & ISRAEL= The institute makes no secret of its extensive links with Israel, AMERICAN INTEREST IS NOT THEIR CONSIDERATION, OR AGENDA.

BROOKINGS INSTITUTE: Why AIPAC Took Over Brookings :(WINEP) Saban Center for Middle East Policy : Television magnate Haim Saban, famously quoted by the New York Times as saying, "I'm a one-issue guy and my issue is Israel." He also funded and established the Saban Institute for the Study of the American Political System within the University of Tel Aviv.

WINEP's ability to place stories that sway American public opinion toward supporting Israeli objectives is quantitatively revealed by analyzing the number of print media stories developed from WINEP .

IRmep: Israel Lobby Initiates Hispanic Strategy:

The Israel lobby clearly sees Hispanic voters as a new and largely untapped force in American politics in need of leadership harnessed to the American Israel Public Affairs Committee's (AIPAC) foreign policy issue framework.

The Scandal is Bigger Than AIPAC:

It involves AIPAC,AEI,PNAC and events that have been briefly mentioned by MSM

JINSA, CSIS, AEI and AIPAC are all Neoconservative Zionist think tank organizations working together to control US government policy, change laws . (ALL WHITE- ? GROUPS) Is that American?? Not in my book..

BUSH, CLINTON, BUSH/ CHENEY, CLINTON & MCCAIN all paid for puppets for such.

Where are the think tanks for AMERICA and American interest??

WE need and want complete change from such Foreign interest. Obama is the only candidate not accepting money from these powerful FOREIGN INTEREST LOBBIES.

Now, these think tanks will attempt to sway the US into war with Iran.

It is these sources that the present administration, and Past Clinton administration, have cherry picked information from, and called it their intelligence reports from intelligence agencies. (MOSSAD) These foreign interest groups, conduct closed-door meetings with US politicians, and distribute books and other publications rich in toned-down AIPAC ideology. Israeli interest. MCCAIN AND CLINTON are top of the list. Party makes no difference. Both have COMMITMENTS!! (GLOBAL ORGANIZED CRIME--JEWISH RUSSIAN MAFIA) YEA--SO!!

These Think Tanks are made up of all white Jews, with the number one issue being Israel. How fair is that? How diverse is that? Then all is kept silent, and behind closed doors. Where is the transparency?

We know the prejudice of this present administration, but realize it has also been the support of the Clintons, McCain, Pelosi, Reid, and many others.

Look at the coalition of our elected senators that end up Israeli senators. Schumer, Lieberman, L. Graham, J. McCain, and Clinton, enough history exists to verify it.

Race has and does make a difference to these people and their policies. Pay attention at home, and internationally. Look at all the human rights violations & issues. Who is responsible, and who does nothing about it? WHO gets all the foreign aid, or more than half for 2% of the population?

Question, and take action. First vote accordingly

Who really is fighting for change and our (Americas) interest & security first

Shouldn't we be thinking for ourselves a little??

How does Clinton's $350 Million pork barrel spending to these special interest groups, help our economy???

DEAR CONCERNED AMERICAN:

Are you fed up with your taxpayer dollars being doled out to foreign governments that openly undermine American ideals and interests?

Well, that's exactly what's happening in the case of Israel.

Despite receiving hundreds of millions of dollars in U.S. taxpayer-funded aid, Israel has begun a full-scale assault on the rule of law with brazen disregard for legal contracts with Western governments, values or firms. Worse, the Israeli government is "shaking down" Western private sector companies that do business in the Middle East. Through lobbies, corruption, campaign financing, and undermining American's rights by intimidating officials into relinquishing the rule of law, to their enterprises & government.. As if Israel's disregard for the rule of law and property rights weren't bad enough, here's the kicker: The hundreds of millions of dollars in U.S. foreign aid to ISRAEL -- care of American taxpayers -- IS GOING TO DIRECTLY BENEFIT THE RUSSIAN JEWISH MAFIA.

WHAT if the phone rings at 3:00AM? FBI has warrants for the corrupt officials involved in syndicate activities. Opinions have it, that all but Obama would flea the Country ~!!

How many more assassinations will Israel & their mafia get away with?? Politicians, business men, journalist, judges & lawyers!

A SERIOUS PEACE
STRATEGY EMERGES:

In 2006 we elected a Congress to end the occupation of Iraq. If we don't hold Congress to it, we will not have the power in 2008 to elect anyone for any stated purpose. Fulfillment of campaign promises will be entirely optional in 2009. Our last chance to hold the current Congress to its commitment is in the coming month of April, when the House takes up Bush's request for another $102 billion of our grandchildren's money.

Foreign lobby controls on our government, of course after killing the opposition.

They had to get rid of the Catholic President, then his brother Attorney General Robert Kennedy. They had put a big dent in operations. Next, Dr. Martin Luther King, who was bringing attention to the effects of organized crime on the poor.

Do you see any pattern? AIPAC (Israeli lobby) took over our government.

UN Resolutions vetoed by US.

Vetoes U.S. 1972 - 2006

1972   condemn Israel for the killings of hundreds of people in air raids on Syria and Lebanon.

1973   reaffirm the rights of the Palestinians and called on Israel to withdraw from the occupied territories.

1976   condemn Israel for attacking Lebanese civilians.

1976   condemn Israel for building settlements in the occupied territories.

1976   call for self-determination for the Palestinians.

1976   reaffirm the rights of the Palestinians.

1978   urged the permanent members (US, USSR, UK, France, China) to ensure the decisions of the United Nations in the maintenance of International Peace and Security.

1978   Criticizes living conditions of the Palestinians.

1978   condemn violation of human rights in the occupied territories of Palestine.

1978   call on the developed countries to increase the quantity and quality of development assistance to underdeveloped countries.

1979   call to end all military and nuclear collaboration with the apartheid regime in South Africa.

1979   Strengthen the arms embargo against South Africa.

1979   Offer assistance to all the oppressed people of South Africa and its liberation movement.

1979   Show concern for the negotiations on disarmament and cessation of the arms race.

1979   call to allow the return of all inhabitants expelled by Israel.

1979   call on Israel to desist from human rights violations.

Report Calls 1979 run of the living conditions of Palestinians in occupied Arab countries.

1979   Provide assistance to the Palestinian people.

1979 Talk sovereignty of national resources in the occupied Arab territories.

1979 call for the protection of exports from developing countries.

1979 call to seek alternative approaches within the United Nations system to enhance the enjoyment of human rights and fundamental freedoms.

1979 Opposes support intervention in the internal or external affairs of states.

Call to a 1979 United Nations Conference on Women.

Including the 1979 Palestinian women in the United Nations Conference on Women.

1979 Safeguarding the right of developing countries in multinational trade negotiations.

1980 Sue Israel to return displaced persons to their homes.

1980 Condemn Israeli policy with regard to the living conditions of the Palestinian people.

1980 condemn the practices of Israeli violations of human rights in the occupied territories. 3 resolutions.

1980 reaffirm the right of self-determination for the Palestinian people.

1980 Providing help the oppressed people of South Africa and their national liberation movement.

1980 Trying to establish a new international economic order to promote the growth of underdeveloped countries and international economic cooperation.

1980 Support Programme of Action for the Second Half of the United Nations Decade for Women.

1980   Declaration of not using nuclear weapons against non-nuclear states.

1980   Emphasize that the development of nations and individuals is a human right.

1980   call for the cessation of all nuclear testing.

1980   Call for implementació n of the Declaration on the Granting of Independence to Colonial Countries and Peoples.

1981   Promote cooperative movements in developing countries.

1981   reaffirm the right of each state to choose its economic and social system in accordance with the wish of its people, without external interference in any form.

1981   condemn the activities of foreign economic interests in the colonial.

1981   call for the cessation of all nuclear weapon tests.

1981   call to action in support of measures to prevent nuclear war, curb the arms race and promote disarmament.

1981   Focus on negotiations for the prohibition of chemical and biological weapons.

1981   Declaring that education, employment, health care, adequate nutrition, development, and so forth. Are human rights.

1981   South Africa Orders for attacking neighboring states, condemns apartheid and calls for tougher sanctions. 7 resolutions.

To   condemn the 1981 coup attempt by South Africa in the Seychelles.

1981   condemn Israel for the treatment of the Palestinians, the violation of human rights and the bombing of Iraq. 18 resolutions.

Condemning the 1982 Israeli invasion of Lebanon. 6 resolutions (1982 to 1983).

1982 Condemning the killing of 11 Muslims in a chapel in Jerusalem by an Israeli soldier.

1982 Call for Israel to withdraw from the Golan Heights occupied in 1967.

1982 condemn apartheid and called for the cessation of economic aid to South Africa. 4 resolutions.

Call 1982 to establish a Global Charter for the protection of the ecology.

Establish a 1982 conference of the United Nations with regard to the state-owned archives and debts.

1982 bans nuclear testing and negotiations and outer space free of nuclear weapons. 3 resolutions.

1982 Supporting a new world order of information and communications.

1982 Prohibition of chemical and bacteriological weapons.

Development of a 1982 law.

1982 Protect against products harmful to health and the environment.

1982 Declaring that education, employment, health care, proper nutrition, national development, as human rights.

1982 Protect against products harmful to health and the environment.

1982 Development of energy sources in developing countries.

1983 Resolutions on apartheid, nuclear arms, economics and international law. 15 resolutions.

1984 Orders support of South Africa in Namibia and other policies.

1984 Lllamar to international action to eliminate apartheid.

1984 condemn Israel for attack and occupy southern Lebanon.

1984 Resolutions on apartheid, nuclear arms, economics and international law. 18 resolutions.

1985 condemn Israel for attack and occupy southern Lebanon.

1985 condemn Israel for using excessive force in the occupied territories.

1985 Resolutions on cooperation, human rights, trade and development. 3 resolutions.

1985 Measures to be taken against Nazi, fascist and neo-fascist activities.

1986 Called on all governments (including the United States) to comply with international law.

1986 Imposing economic and military sanctions against South Africa.

1986 condemn Israel for its actions against Lebanese civilians.

1986 call on Israel to respect Muslim holy places.

1986 condemn Israel for abducting a Libyan transport plane.

1986 Resolutions on cooperation, security, human rights, trade, media, environment and development. 8 resolutions.

1987 call on Israel to comply with the Geneva Convention in its treatment of Palestinians.

1987 call on Israel to stop deporting Palestinians.

1987 condemn Israel for its actions in Lebanon. 2 resolutions.

1987 call on Israel to withdraw its forces from Lebanon.

1987 Cooperation between the United Nations and the League of Arab States.

1987 call for compliance in the International Court of Justice concerning the military and paramilitary activities against Nicaragua and a call to end the trade embargo against Nicaragua. 2 resolutions.

1987 Measures to prevent international terrorism, study of the causes and economic policies that emphasize terrorism, agrees a conference to define terrorism and distinguish it from the struggle of peoples for national liberation.

1987 Resolutions on the journalism, debt and international trade. 3 resolutions.

Opposition to the 1987 figure of weapons in space.

1987 Opposition to the development of new weapons of mass destruction.

Opposition to the 1987 nuclear tests. 2 resolutions.

1987 proposal to establish in the South Atlantic a "Zone of Peace."

1988 Orders practices Israelis against the Palestinians in the occupied territories. 5 resolutions (1988 and 1989).

1989 Condemn U.S. invasion To Panama.

1989 Orders of US troops Pillaging by the Nicaraguan ambassador's residence in Panama.

1989 Orders support from US To the Contra army in Nicaragua.

1989   condemn the embargo illegal US Nicaragua.

1989   was opposed to the acquisition of territory by force.

       Call 1989 for a resolution to the Arab-Israeli conflict based on previous resolutions of the UN.

1990   Mail-three observers of the Security Council to the occupied territories.

       Reaffirms 1995 that the territories of East Jerusalem annexed by Israel is occupied territory.

1997   calls on Israel to stop building settlements in East Jerusalem and other occupied territories. 2 resolutions.

       Calls to USA 1999 To end its trade embargo against Cuba. 8 resolutions (1992 to 1999).

2001   To send unarmed monitors to the West Bank and the Gaza Strip.

       Condemns Israel for acts of terror against civilians in the occupied territories.

       To set up the International Criminal Court.

2002   To renew the peace keeping mission in Bosnia.

2002   Condemns the killing of UK worker for the United Nations by Israeli forces. Condemns the destruction of the World Food Programme warehouse.

2003   Condemns a decision by the Israeli parliament to "remove" the elected Palestinian president, Yasser Arafat. Condemns the building of a wall by Israel on Palestinian land.

2003   To end the USA's 40 year embargo of Cuba. 179-3

2004   Condemns the assassination of Hamas leader, Sheik Ahmad Yassin.

2004   Condemns the Israeli incursion and killings in Gaza.

2004   Production and processing of weapon-usable material should be under international control.

2006   Calls for an end to Israeli military incursions and attacks on Gaza.

John McCain and Hillary Clinton campaigns are set up to fool the public into thinking we have options... when they are working for the same boss. We are supposed to be the employer of the president, but unfortunately, corporations and the Israeli lobby (AIPAC) are the bosses of both candidates. Our only option to beat this strangle hold is Barrack Obama. Vote for Change.

Thank GOD for Jeffery Toobin! At least he had the guts to call McCain & Clinton on this last attack. We need to continue to push CNN to cover this issue appropriately, and call it for what it is. An attempt by Clinton & McCain to try to portray Barack as something he absolutely is NOT...elitist.

Media was reporting all kinds of wild stories that "Obama is out of the race" and "It's over" all while taking one little tiny snippet of what he said and spinning it. Is that what a news organization is supposed to do?

They have played this game for months and we are asking you all to help out, if you can, just for a minute. Call their viewer comment line and leave a message about their disgraceful "yellow" journalism of misleading viewers and distorting the facts. Twisting and spinning the truth out of proportion.

PALESTINE, IRAQ, LEBANON, SYRIA, LYBIA, EGYPT, JORDAN, AND IRAN

The "Whole World is Wrong"---Bush, Zionism, and Israel are right?? Who agrees?

Bush support has now increased to 11% in America, I guess he still has hope.

Persistent aggressions by the Zionists are making life more and more difficult for the rightful owners of the land of Palestine. In broad day-light, in front of cameras and before the eyes of the world, they are bombarding innocent defenseless civilians, bulldozing houses, firing machine guns at students in the streets and alleys, and subjecting their families to endless grief.

No day goes by without a new crime.

Palestinian mothers, just like Iranian and American mothers, love their children, and are painfully bereaved by the imprisonment, wounding and murder of their children. What mother wouldn't?

For 60 years, the Zionist regime has driven millions of the inhabitants of Palestine out of their homes. Many of these refugees have died in the Diaspora and in refugee camps. Their children have spent their youth in these camps and are aging while still in the hope of returning to homeland.

You know well that the US administration has persistently provided blind and blanket support to the Zionist regime, has emboldened it to continue its crimes, and has prevented the UN Security Council from condemning it.

Who can deny such broken promises and grave injustices towards humanity by the US administration?

Governments are there to serve their own people. No people want to side with or support any oppressors. But regrettably, the US administration disregards even its own public opinion and remains in the forefront of supporting the trampling of the rights of the Palestinian people.

Let's take a look at Iraq . Since the commencement of the US military presence in Iraq , hundreds of thousands of Iraqis have been killed, maimed or displaced. Terrorism in Iraq has grown exponentially. With the presence of the US military in Iraq , nothing has been done to rebuild the ruins, to restore the infrastructure or to alleviate poverty. The US Government used the pretext of the existence of weapons of mass destruction in Iraq , but later it became clear that that was just a lie and a deception.

Although Saddam was overthrown and people are happy about his departure, the pain and suffering of the Iraqi people has persisted and has even been aggravated.

In Iraq , about one hundred and fifty thousand American soldiers, separated from their families and loved ones, are operating under the command of the current US administration. A substantial number of them have been killed or wounded and their presence in Iraq has tarnished the image of the American people and government.

Their mothers and relatives have, on numerous occasions, displayed their discontent with the presence of their sons and daughters in a land thousands of miles away from US shores. American soldiers often wonder why they have been sent to Iraq .

We consider it extremely unlikely that , the American people, consent to the billions of dollars of annual expenditure from our treasury for this military misadventure.

Noble Americans,

We have heard that the US administration is kidnapping its presumed opponents from across the globe and arbitrarily holding them without trial or any international supervision in horrendous prisons that it has established in various parts of the world. God knows who these detainees actually are, and what terrible fate awaits them.

We have certainly heard the sad stories of the Guantanamo and Abu-Ghraib prisons. The US administration attempts to justify them through its proclaimed "war on terror." But every one knows that such behavior, in fact, offends global public opinion, exacerbates resentment and thereby spreads terrorism, and tarnishes the US image and its credibility among nations.

The US administration's illegal and immoral behavior is not even confined to outside its borders. We are witnessing daily that under the pretext of "the war on terror," civil liberties in the United States are being increasingly curtailed. Even the privacy of individuals is fast losing its meaning. Judicial due process and fundamental rights are trampled upon. Private phones are tapped, suspects are arbitrarily arrested, sometimes beaten in the streets, or even shot to death.

We have no doubt that the American people do not approve of this behavior and indeed deplore it.

The US administration does not accept accountability before any organization, institution or council. The US administration has undermined the credibility of international organizations, particularly the United Nations and its Security Council. But, we do not intend to address all the challenges and calamities in this message.

The legitimacy, power and influence of a government do not emanate from its arsenals of tanks, fighter aircrafts, missiles or nuclear weapons. Legitimacy and influence reside in sound logic, quest for justice and compassion and empathy for all humanity. The global position of the United States is in all probability weakened because the administration has continued to resort to force, to conceal the truth, and to mislead the American people about its policies and practices.

Undoubtedly, the American people are not satisfied with this behavior and they showed their discontent in the recent elections. We hope that in the wake of the mid-term elections, the administration of President Bush will have heard and will heed the message of the American people.

Our questions are the following:

Is there not a better approach to governance?

Is it not possible to put wealth and power in the service of peace, stability, prosperity and the happiness of all peoples through a commitment to justice and respect for the rights of all nations, instead of aggression and war?

We all condemn terrorism, because its victims are the innocent.

But, can terrorism be contained and eradicated through war, destruction and the killing of hundreds of thousands of innocents?

If that were possible, then why has the problem not been resolved?

The sad experience of invading Iraq is before us all.

What has blind support for the Zionists by the US administration brought for the American people? It is regrettable that for the US administration, the interests of these occupiers supersedes the interests of the American people and of the other nations of the world.

What have the Zionists done for the American people that the US administration considers itself obliged to blindly support these infamous aggressors? Is it not because they have imposed themselves on a substantial portion of the banking, financial, cultural and media sectors?

We recommend that in a demonstration of respect for the American people and for humanity, the right of Palestinians to live in their own homeland should be recognized so that millions of Palestinian refugees can return to their homes and the future of all of Palestine and its form of government be determined in a referendum. This will benefit everyone.

Now that Iraq has a Constitution and an independent Assembly and Government, would it not be more beneficial to bring the US officers and soldiers home, and to spend the astronomical US military expenditures in Iraq for the welfare and prosperity of the American people? As you know very well, many victims of Katrina continue to suffer, and countless Americans continue to live in poverty and homelessness.

We also like to say a word to the winners of the recent elections in the US :

The United States has had many administrations; some who have left a positive legacy, and others that are neither remembered fondly by the American people nor by other nations.

Now that you control an important branch of the US Government, you will also be held to account by the people and by history.

If the US Government meets the current domestic and external challenges with an approach based on truth and Justice, it can remedy some of the past afflictions and alleviate some of the global resentment and hatred of America . But if the approach remains the same, it would not be unexpected that the American people would similarly reject the new electoral winners, although the recent elections, rather than reflecting a victory, in reality point to the failure of the current administration's policies. These issues had been extensively dealt with in my letter to President Bush earlier this year.

To sum up:

It is possible to govern based on an approach that is distinctly different from one of coercion, force and injustice.

It is possible to sincerely serve and promote common human values, and honesty and compassion.

It is possible to provide welfare and prosperity without tension, threats, imposition or war.

It is possible to lead the world towards the aspired perfection by adhering to unity, monotheism, morality and spirituality and drawing upon the teachings of the Divine Prophets.

Then, the American people, who are God-fearing and followers of Divine religions, will overcome every difficulty.

What we stated represents some of our anxieties and concerns.

We are confident , the American people, will play an instrumental role in the establishment of justice and spirituality throughout the world. The promises of the Almighty and His prophets will certainly be realized; Justice and Truth will prevail and all nations will live a true life in a climate replete with love, compassion and fraternity.

The US governing establishment, the authorities and the powerful should not choose irreversible paths. As all prophets have taught us, injustice and transgression will eventually bring about decline and demise. Today, the path of return to faith and spirituality is open and unimpeded.

We should all heed the Divine Word.

We pray to the Almighty to bless the Iranian and American nations and indeed all nations of the world with dignity and success.

Do not "underestimate" the "anger," "frustration," and "determination," of your citizens who demand "justice and fairness."

For too long, policies that support Israeli militarism and occupation have gone unchallenged. Political voices raising even minor disagreements with prevailing policies are silenced or subject to campaigns of intimidation. We must open the door to full debate regarding U.S. relationship with Israel and U.S. policy with other countries in the region.

NO MORE PUBLIC FUNDS, TAX DOLLARS, FOR ISRAEL SUPPORT!

We as citizens of the United States request that no further funding of a religious state with Our public funds continue. We request that no further military aid be given to a religious state. We also request a return of our funds. From the "Jewish State of Israel".
Our constitution specifically separates church & state. NONE of our tax dollars should be used in support of any religious institution, government or annex of such state.

They may have declared themselves a separate State, but our constitution strictly forbids using our public money or tax dollars from supporting such, and we demand that such practice discontinue immediately.

William H. Rehnquist spoke for the court:

Both tax exemptions and tax deductibility are a form of subsidy that is administered through the tax system. A tax exemption has much the same effect as cash grant to the organization of the amount of tax it would have to pay on its income.

The significance of this decision is often overlooked. If tax exemption is a form of subsidy, then church property tax exemption is a clear violation of the establishment clause of the First Amendment. All that is necessary to make church property tax exemption a thing of the past is for an irate taxpayer who is tired of high taxes to file suit to force churches to pay their "fair share."

Tenth Circuit Court addressed, and held that "tax exemption is a privilege, a matter of grace rather than a right."

The question of tax exemption for churches is clear: the foundation has been laid for taxing church property and perhaps even church income.

As the budget deficits of the federal, state and local government's increase, the possibility of taxing church property also rises -- despite the long history of tax exemption.

We are sick and tired of the "Zionist-Movement" the cost of the "WAR" they demanded, the amount of holdings & investments rather then any amount of return to the community. The threat of Falwell to use 200,000 preachers to preach his message from the pulpit is not only wrong it is unlimited use of propaganda!

The millions spent on foolish campaigns designed to shape or change public opinion in regard to this or that: divorce, birth control, the falseness of the Darwinian Theory, or almost anything in connection with science and history! The blather about saints and cures and bringing all to Jesus, the while taxes are evaded and the scummy politicians whom they endorse, or even nominate and elect to office, proceed to rob the public in favor of the corporations and churches whom they serve! No wonder ignorance, no wonder illusion, when those with power in the religious field knowingly delude and mislead the masses! The things told them! That it is important to vote for this or that crook; uphold religion; it is good for the people to go to war, to put religion in the schools, to give into the hands of these mental bandits the care and education of all children, so that they may be properly enslaved by religion! (A slave, in my opinion, is the man who does not think for himself. A man with knowledge is not powerless.) But always, with suave and polished words.

How about a Robertson or Bush Whisper! God has told me, and I will tell you, and you shall follow and sustain me as my servant who am the servant of God! SURE!

One would think from that that the Churches were a branch of the Government, a public institution, whereas they are only semipublic, being under the control of a special group of patrons, and as such should be taxed and made to pay the same as any other self-aggrandizing corporation.

The State now should not permit them to go tax free, and should, should it not? enjoy and participate in any money-making of this nature, which is certainly no legitimate function of religion. Then look close at the MONEY!!

Well now, church buildings alone in America, without parsonages, investments, securities, schools, orphanages, hospitals and monasteries, are valued in the trillions. Investments such as in Defense etc, also will be in the trillions. Do they ever cough up in crisis,

No they just manage the money from the congregation they solicit it from. Lets call it Alms instead of Tyethings. America now represented by the money-mad leaders who are dictating not only the economics but the philosophy of the country and using the religionists to help them. Or might it be the fool led by fools.

We will sue for tax fairness due to the last six years of Church involvement in Politics, openly judging people with a different political view, telling a congregation they must support the Republican Party, and support an unjust "WAR".

Now pay for it, I left the Church because I'm proud to be a Democrat, American, a Christian, but no longer a member of any denomination that supports corruption and/or WAR. BLAME THE PAT ROBERTSONS AND JERRY FALWELLS FOR INVOLVING CHURCH & STATE.

" A preacher of the gospel ought not to be patiently listened to those, who eloquently promotes the blessings of liberty or occupation by WAR ,as if they make them free, while in fact hold their fellow-humans, administer torture, death and destruction. Take their property and resources in a most dreadful and lacerating bondage." Might that be the precise reasoning for separation of Church & State?

NOW IMPEACH, AND HOLD THOSE ACCOUNTABLE FOR THEIR CRIMES AND HYPOCRACY!!

Due to the current crisis, approximately 2,000 Iraqis are forced to flee their homes every day. More than 2.2 million Iraqis have already fled to neighboring countries such as Syria and Jordan, where they face a daily struggle to survive. Jordan has closed its borders, and Syria plans to next month. Soon, Iraqis threatened with death will literally have no way to flee.

The atrocities are just coming to light in Congress, but have been in sight for 4 years by many..

The government has silenced media that wasn't already in their pocket. Or again was that Blackwater doing the administrations dirty work.

But of course they get immunity!! 128 Journalist have been killed in Iraq.

Mr. Bush refuses to talk with the Iranian government directly, and instead sends aircraft carriers and gives orders for our troops to kill Iranian "operatives" in Iraq, even while the Iraqi government invites representatives from its neighbor to join them in security talks.

This is insane, and a war with Iran would be even more catastrophic than the war in Iraq. It would bring the condemnation of the world down on us, increase attacks on U.S. troops in Iraq, and continue to increase the terrorist threat – as the war in Iraq itself has done.

Generations to come will look to this moment to see whether our government chose diplomacy, sanity and peace, or unending war. Please let me know what you intend to do about this.

Contrary to what some may believe, the Bush Administration's failure in Iraq hasn't disencouraged the U.S. to launch a new war in the Middle East.

The Israeli interests have become the main factor defining the U.S. agenda in the region, which makes the Jewish state the only partner capable of persuading or forcing the U.S. to abandon its decision of invading Iran.

Only a change in the Zionists' strategy can change the U.S. plans to attack Iran, so argued Scott Ritter, the former weapons inspector, in his new book, Target Iran: The Truth about White House's Plan for Regime Change.

"One of the big problems is — and here goes the grenade — Israel. The second you mention the word 'Israel,' the nation Israel, the concept Israel, many in the American press become very defensive. And the other thing we're not allowed to do is discuss the notion that Israel and the notion of Israeli interests may in fact be dictating what America is doing, that what we're doing in the Middle East may not be to the benefit of America's national security, but to Israel's national security,"

The lobby that Israel and its supporters have built in the United States to make all this aid happen, and to ban discussion of it from the national dialogue, goes far beyond AIPAC, with its $15 million budget, its 150 employees, and its five or six registered lobbyists who manage to visit every member of Congress individually once or twice a year.

AIPAC, in turn, can draw upon the resources of the Conference of Presidents of Major American Jewish Organizations, a roof group set up solely to coordinate the efforts of some 52 national Jewish organizations on behalf of Israel.

AIPAC, or the American Israel Public Affairs Committee, describes itself as the most important organization affecting the U.S. relationship with Israel. With a budget of $65 million, and membership now standing at over 100,000, it is no wonder that congressional staffers consider it one of the most powerful and effective lobbies on Capitol Hill.

This conundrum should have diplomats, parliamentarians, and foreign ministries huddled in their back rooms trying to sort out their own positions, rather than attempting to starve the Palestinians into Hamas's capitulation. For it is not only the funding freeze that has become rampant nonsense. The entire Road Map logic has become nonsense, too.

Zionists have betrayed all of this, and that is a tragedy not just for Jews, but for all of us.

Did the Jews of the Old Testament come from what is now Israel? The answer is No.

"People who occupied some land two thousand years ago for a historically brief period, to the detriment of those who have been there since."

"Israel was established on the basis of theft. The State of Israel is Satan's offspring - a satanic offspring. It was founded on theft from the first moment. It was founded on the basis of robbery, terror, killing, torture, assassination, death, stealing land and killing people and will continue this way, never able to exist because its birth was unnatural, a satanic offspring, and cannot exist among human beings...

It cannot exist naturally, like other nations in this world."

"Our position is that even if the Zionist State [Israel] is the size of a postage stamp it has no right to exist. Occupied Palestine must be decolonized, deracialized and restored to the Palestinian people as a single sovereign state. In plain English, the Zionist State must be dismantled."

"All Palestine should be returned to the Palestinians and other occupied lands should be returned to their owners. And the Zionist enterprise should cease to exist. Only then will the misery wrought by Zionism disappear."

This may take some people by surprise, but the UN has not used the term "Jewish state" since 1947. Resolution 181 then called for a "Jewish state" and an "Arab state," with gerrymandered borders designed to craft Jewish and Arab majorities in each state. But the attempt was rendered obsolete when Zionist forces established "Israel" on a much greater swath of territory that had, in total, held a substantial Arab majority, and expelled most of the Arab residents. As refugees, according to the Geneva Conventions, those Arab residents have the right to return to their homes, villages, towns and cities. But their return would eliminate the Jewish majority in what became "Israel," so Israel hasn't allowed this.

Hence the UN cannot confirm Israel as a Jewish state (i.e., a state that can legitimately sustain a Jewish majority) without contradicting international law regarding the right of refugees. When the UN refers to "Israel" today, it does not understand Israel as the "Jewish state" in the old ethnic-majority terms of 1947, because Israel can be granted no "right" to an ethnic demography that would prevent the return of refugees.

Also, times have simply changed. In 1947, ethnic nationalism still made some belated sense, although it was already discredited by the dreadful abuses wreaked by Germany and Japan. Today, recognizing the "right" of any state to compose itself legally as an ethnic-majority state would clearly flout UN conventions on human rights and non-discrimination. The UN and EU therefore cannot openly endorse Israel's right to compose itself as one. It would make hash of international efforts in Rwanda, the Sudan, Kashmir, Afghanistan, Kosovo, and many other crisis spots.

So the US has lured the EU, Canada, and Norway into a trap. If they hold that Hamas must recognize Israel as a Jewish state (with a right to preserve an ethnic-Jewish majority), then they must state clearly that it endorses ethnic-majority governance. But those they cannot explicitly endorse Israel's right to ethnocracy, because it would contradict international law as well as its own diplomacy in a host of other conflict zones, so on what grounds does they require Hamas to do so?

THE CRIME FAMILY STRATEGY:

THE CRIME FAMILY STRATEGY !!

As Bill Clinton keeps telling us, Hillary and John McCain are close friends. That relationship goes much deeper then friends.

They are and have been a big part of the corruption in Washington. Both are deeply committed to AIPAC and the Jewish mafia.

The Clinton's know that the primary has been lost to Obama. BUT they know they have to stay in the race to tear Obama down. They will continue the attacks, smear Obama and distroy the party for the benefit of their special interest groups. Foreign lobby, and corporate corruption. They are now in the race for the benefit of their comrad & partner in crime. John McCain.

Watch how the media will play along with the same game. Owned and controlled by members of the same Organized Crime Family.

That America is the control of government we need change from, it no longer matters which party. Both parties are influenced by the money and agenda of AIPAC & comrads.

Clinton was favored by the Organization to WIN, but Now that she is not going to win. John McCain is their candidate. The Clinton's have to stay in and attack & smear. OR!!

Pain and suffering around the world such as Poverty, Hunger, medical attention, shelter, and security, are things the USA government and rich religious leaders ignore.

They concentrate on WAR for profit, investments in defense contractors, any things legal or illegal to make profits for themselves and their close associates.

Associates that advise them help run their campaigns; raise the funds from lobbies and corporations to keep the corrupt in office.

Why all the attacks on Obama. It is because he represents something different. A change from the old policies, and polarized practices; of 60 years.

Obama will be President for the American people; he will be accountable to the American people. NOT the organized crime syndicate that has had Control of Washington & beyond.

The UN has the power to make a difference, and needs to unify & exercise such power.

MAKE YOUR VOICE HEARD!
CHANGE THE WAY THINGS ARE
DONE IN THIS COUNTRY!

Former CIA counterterrorism specialist Philip Giraldi, comparing the propaganda campaign against Iran to that which preceded the war on Iraq, has recently declared, "It is absolutely parallel."

Unfortunately the Congress dominated by opportunist elected in a popular expression of antiwar sentiment have not taken a firm stance against an attack on Iran based on lies. Simply stated they are again controlled by a foreign lobby and their special interest MONEY .

Uri Lubrani, senior advisor to "Defense" Minister Amir Peretz, tells the Jewish Agency's Board of Governors that the U.S. "does not understand the threat and has not done enough," and therefore "must be shaken awake." We must have another 911 incident.

Tira urges the Lobby ((AIPAC) to turn to "potential presidential candidates. . . so that they support immediate action against Iran.

Many Americans would find such statements deeply offensive in their arrogance and condescension. President Bush has indeed been weakened by the "Iraq failure" Tira acknowledges, arising from a war that the Lobby demanded with enormous enthusiasm.

So now, the Israeli war advocates avert, the U.S. president needs to be helped to do the right thing and attack Iran by foreign lobbyists who will use their power to force the fools in the present congress & senate, especially presidential candidates.

Hillary Clinton & John McCain have appeared at their convention, and have accepted their blood money for their campaigns. They are being sucked in again, the same as Iraq. "Israel doesn't want peace!"

You can't steal land, create gains from war-related industries, oppress others and then expect peace.

Now the concern turns to the unexpected success of the Obama campaign. The media attack dogs become more and more necessary to smear Obama any way possible. Voter beware of the real deceptions coming.

Candidates can be and are bought by special interest money, AIPAC & comrads.

Media is also owned by the same people.

The voters can not be bought, only deceived for periods of time. You can deceive some of the people all the time, all the people some of the time. BUT not all the people all the time.

We will not be deceived in 2008, Obama will be president 2009.

"Words are a form of action, capable of influencing change." What this country needs is a president not only with experience and knowledge - which both Hillary Clinton and Barack Obama possess - but a president with a vision of the future, and the persuasive ability to make that vision come true. Words are not just words when they come from Sen. Obama. They are actions. Words WITH-OUT DECEPTION.

We must not allow Congress to sleepwalk until the next election. If congressional representatives and senators continue to support the war and keep our troops needlessly in Iraq, then we must publicize their record and hold them accountable in (NOVEMBER).

Do not forget 2006 Mandate, and who did or did not support the American people.

Stop paying for the Military Occupation of Iraq.

NOTICE: MEDIA IGNORS THE INCREASED DEATH RATE OF OUR TROOPS IN IRAQ.

VIOLENCE AGAINST AMERICANS INCREASED OVER THE LAST FEW WEEKS.
THEY WANT TO CALL IT SUCCESS!!

Finally, we want to say a word about the basic decency we have seen in Mr. Obama. Mrs. Clinton continues to throw the Rev. Wright up in his face as part of her mission to keep stoking the fears of White America. Every time she does this we shout at the TV, "Say it, Obama! Say that when she and her husband were having marital difficulties regarding Monica Lewinsky, who she and Bill brought to the White House for 'spiritual counseling?' Answer "THE REVEREND JEREMIAH WRIGHT!"

But no, Obama won't throw that at her. It wouldn't be right. It wouldn't be decent. She's been through enough hurt. And so he remains silent and takes the mud she throws in his face.

OBAMA FOR PRESIDENT:

NOT BOBBLE HEAD THAT SHAKES HER HEAD YES YES TO BUSH FOR 8 YEARS.

We are not looking for a "QUEEN FOR A DAY ONE", we are looking for a President to represent us, the American people , for the next eight years.

Are we as Americans looking forward to change in our government? Change from the past polarized government, and the influence of major foreign & corporate lobbies.

Do we want a president for the people of all 50 states, of the United States? (OR) Do we want a president representing the BIG States, plus an undeclared 51St. state? That receives more of our tax money then any other, which does not comply with international law?

Do we want a president that is by the people, and for the people of America? Not the special interest groups that line their pockets.

WE ASK YOU TO VOTE FOR OBAMA, VOTE FOR REAL CHANGE.

Am I upset with the network coverage of the presidential campaigns? Yes. In fact, you might say I'm bitter. But I'm going to do something about it.

Moderators George Stephanopoulos and Charlie Gibson spent the first 50 minutes obsessed with distractions that only political insiders care about the stale Rev. Wright story,& Obama attacks. They directed a video question to Barack Obama asking if he loves the American flag or not.(Seriously).

Enough is enough. The public needs the media to stop hurting the national dialogue in this important election year.

Media ownership causes bias. AIPAC for Billary.

America wants to hear how our candidates will handle the tough issues, but evidently ABC is more interested in gotcha politics and trumped up gossip.

BUT only on Obama, nothing mentioned about Hillary, campaigning in a Bar room, her saying that is where she would find the unemployed men to talk to about the economy. Then patronizing them by drinking with them, and acting like they need to vote for her. . Transgressors against moral values? How do ministers view such.

Booze money, might be better spent on the family. Ladies certainly don't hang around BAR ROOMS, why would a lady campaign there?

Questions on the economy? Nope. The war? Not really. Global warming? Jobs? $4 gas? Why would America want to know about those things?

We have heard all the attacks on Obama. Now we want answers on "Clinton values", as if there are any.

200,000 BAPTIST MINISTERS, PLUS MANY OTHERS SUPPORT MCCAIN ON "BIBLICAL TERMS"

"To promote a woman to bear rule, superiority, dominion, or empire above any realm, nation, or city, is repugnant to nature; an insult to God, a thing most contrary to his revealed will and approved ordinance; and finally, it is the subversion of good order, of all equity and justice."

"Nature, I say, does paint them forth to be weak, frail, impatient, feeble, and foolish; and experience has declared them to be inconstant, variable, cruel, lacking the spirit of counsel and regiment. And these notable faults have men in all ages espied in that kind, for the which not only they have removed women from rule and authority, but also some have thought that men subject to the counsel or empire of their wives were unworthy of public office. For thus writes Aristotle, in the second of his Politics. What difference shall we put, says he, whether that women bear authority, or the husbands that obey the empire of their wives, be appointed to be magistrates? For what ensues the one, must needs follow the other: to wit, injustice, confusion, and disorder."

"Woman in her greatest perfection was made to serve and obey man, not to rule and command him. As St. Paul does reason in these words: "Man is not of the woman, but the woman of the man. And man was not created for the cause of the woman, but the woman for the cause of man; and therefore ought the woman to have a power upon her head" [1 Cor. 11:8-10] (that is, a cover in sign of subjection). Of which words it is plain that the apostle means, that woman in her greatest perfection should have known that man was lord above her; and therefore that she should never have pretended any kind of superiority above him, no more than do the angels above God the Creator, or above Christ their head. So I say, that in her greatest perfection, woman was created to be subject to man."

On the question of the inferior status and sinful nature of women all theologians of this time, whether Catholic or Protestant, were in agreement!

Prime Example: Congress has never had such a low rating. Look at the attitude of, and the disregard for the people's mandate of 2006. Our issues taken off the table, by this incompatent leader, where is speaker of the house. Now put the presidency in jeopardy the same way?

Could it be worse then Bush. Well look at congress, their rating is even lower then the BUSH/CHENEY administration; did we consider that happening in 2006? Leader of the House, no spine, bows to administration. Take everything off the table.

Hillary's answers so far to any crisis situation is, stop, freeze, don't do anything. Let her study it, let the lobbies determine how to proceed.

That is what the "GREAT SOLUTIONS" WILL BE. Have you heard it? Think any thing else will be her policy. Look at them all lined up already to take over. Remember the CAKE WALK this was going to be for them!

CLINTON CAN NOT WIN IN THE GENERAL ELECTION!!

Washington, DC – The public interest group that investigates and prosecutes government corruption, today released its 2007 list of Washington's " Most Wanted Corrupt Politicians." The list, in alphabetical order, includes:

1. Senator Hillary Rodham Clinton (D-NY): In addition to her long and sordid ethics record, Senator Hillary Clinton took a lot of heat in 2007 – and rightly so – for blocking the release her official White House records. Many suspect these records contain a treasure trove of information related to her role in a number of serious Clinton-era scandals. Moreover, in March 2007, Judicial Watch filed an ethics complaint against Senator Clinton for filing false financial disclosure forms with the U.S. Senate (again). And Hillary's top campaign contributor, Norman Hsu, was exposed as a felon and a fugitive from justice in 2007. Hsu pleaded guilt to one count of grand theft for defrauding investors as part of a multi-million dollar Ponzi scheme.

2. Rep. John Conyers (D-MI): Conyers reportedly repeatedly violated the law and House ethics rules, forcing his staff to serve as his personal servants, babysitters, valets and campaign workers while on the government payroll. While the House Ethics Committee investigated these allegations in 2006, and substantiated a number of the accusations against Conyers, the committee blamed the staff and required additional administrative record-keeping and employee training. Judicial Watch obtained documentation in 2007 from a former Conyers staffer that sheds new light on the activities and conduct on the part of the Michigan congressman, which appear to be at a minimum

inappropriate and likely unlawful. Judicial Watch called on the Attorney General in 2007 to investigate the matter.

3. Senator Larry Craig (R-ID): In one of the most shocking scandals of 2007, Senator Craig was caught by police attempting to solicit sex in a Minneapolis International Airport men's bathroom during the summer. Senator Craig reportedly "sent signals" to a police officer in an adjacent stall that he wanted to engage in sexual activity. When the police officer showed Craig his police identification under the bathroom stall divider and pointed toward the exit, the senator reportedly exclaimed 'No!'" When asked to produce identification, Craig presented police his U.S. Senate business card and said, "What do you think of that?" The power play didn't work. Craig was arrested, charged and entered a guilty plea. Despite enormous pressure from his Republican colleagues to resign from the Senate, Craig refused.

4. Senator Diane Feinstein (D-CA): As a member of the Senate Appropriations Committee's subcommittee on military construction, Feinstein reviewed military construction government contracts, some of which were ultimately awarded to URS Corporation and Perini, companies then owned by Feinstein's husband, Richard Blum. While the Pentagon ultimately awards military contracts, there is a reason for the review process. The Senate's subcommittee on Military Construction's approval carries weight. Sen. Feinstein, therefore, likely had influence over the decision making process. Senator Feinstein also attempted to undermine ethics reform in 2007, arguing in favor of a perk that allows members of Congress to book multiple airline flights and then cancel them without financial penalty. Judicial Watch's investigation into this matter is ongoing.

5. Former New York Mayor Rudy Giuliani (R-NY): Giuliani came under fire in late 2007 after it was discovered the former New York mayor's office "billed obscure city agencies for tens of thousands of dollars in security expenses amassed during the time when he was beginning an extramarital relationship with

future wife Judith Nathan in the Hamptons..." ABC News also reported that Giuliani provided Nathan with a police vehicle and a city driver at taxpayer expense. All of this news came on the heels of the federal indictment on corruption charges of Giuliani's former Police Chief and business partner Bernard Kerik, who pleaded guilty in 2006 to accepting a $165,000 bribe in the form of renovations to his Bronx apartment from a construction company attempting to land city contracts.

6. Governor Mike Huckabee (R-AR): Governor Huckabee enjoyed a meteoric rise in the polls in December 2007, which prompted a more thorough review of his ethics record. According to The Associated Press: "[Huckabee's] career has also been colored by 14 ethics complaints and a volley of questions about his integrity, ranging from his management of campaign cash to his use of a nonprofit organization to subsidize his income to his destruction of state computer files on his way out of the governor's office." And what was Governor Huckabee's response to these ethics allegations? Rather than cooperating with investigators, Huckabee sued the state ethics commission twice and attempted to shut the ethics process down.

7. I. Lewis "Scooter" Libby: Libby, former Chief of Staff to Vice President Dick Cheney, was sentenced to 30 months in prison and fined $250,000 for lying and obstructing the Valerie Plame CIA leak investigation. Libby was found guilty of four felonies -- two counts of perjury, one count of making false statements to the FBI and one count of obstructing justice – all serious crimes. Unfortunately, Libby was largely let off the hook. In an appalling lack of judgment, President Bush issued "Executive Clemency" to Libby and commuted the sentence.

8. Rep. Nancy Pelosi (D-CA): House Speaker Nancy Pelosi, who promised a new era of ethics enforcement in the House of Representatives, snuck a $25 million gift to her husband, Paul Pelosi, in a $15 billion Water Resources Development Act recently passed by Congress. The pet project involved renovating

ports in Speaker Pelosi's home base of San Francisco. Pelosi just happens to own apartment buildings near the areas targeted for improvement, and will almost certainly experience a significant boost in property value as a result of Pelosi's earmark. Earlier in the year, Pelosi found herself in hot water for demanding access to a luxury Air Force jet to ferry the Speaker and her entourage back and forth from San Francisco non-stop, in unprecedented request which was wisely rejected by the Pentagon. And under Pelosi's leadership, the House ethics process remains essentially shut down – which protects members in both parties from accountability.

9. Senator Harry Reid (D-NV): Over the last few years, Reid has been embroiled in a series of scandals that cast serious doubt on his credibility as a self-professed champion of government ethics, and 2007 was no different. According to The Los Angeles Times, over the last four years, Reid has used his influence in Washington to help a developer, Havey Whittemore, clear obstacles for a profitable real estate deal. As the project advanced, the Times reported, "Reid received tens of thousands of dollars in campaign contributions from Whittemore." Whittemore also hired one of Reid's sons (Leif) as his personal lawyer and then promptly handed the junior Reid the responsibility of negotiating the real estate deal with federal officials. Leif Reid even called his father's office to talk about how to obtain the proper EPA permits, a clear conflict of interest.

10. Senator John McCain (R-Arz): McCain dumped his first wife after she had been disabled in an auto accident. Although this woman had worked tirelessly to get him released from captivity, he did not hesitate to betray her with other women upon finding her crippled when he returned home. In fact, McCain has racked up quite a reputation as a womanizer. This time he was determined to do it right. Since he had no fortune of his own, he acquired one through his second marriage. Sampley writes that the senator's net worth is "possibly as much as $1.2 million or more, excluding personal residences … McCain listed

his [second] wife, Cindy, as the source of most of his assets. . ."
According to the Phoenix Gazette of May 19, 1987, "the bulk
of McCain's assets consisted of stock in the Glendale firms --
Hensley & Co., a beer distributorship headed by his father-in-
law; Western Leasing Co., which leases trucks and equipment;
and Eagle Enterprises, which invests in real estate and stock." In
fact, the senator married the daughter of one of the richest men
in Arizona. It seems that McCain got more than just a wife in
the bargain, he married into a family that already had quite a
reputation in that state. Since family ties are always somewhat
convoluted and difficult to track. The candidate had been seen
from time to time in the company of "Jewish gangsters." John
McCain, like the Clinton's, made his Faustian bargain in order to
have a career in politics. It wasn't the first he had made, nor was
it his last. If we continue to put such people at the head of our
government, in time the entire country will become as rotten as
Arkansas and Arizona already are. Kemper Marley, the Arizona
godfather, certainly didn't lack for connections. Marley had a
slick mouthpiece who kept him in the clear. The lawyer's name is
William Rehnquist, who was the Chief Justice of the Supreme
Court. Mind you, I'm not suggesting that there is anything shady
about lawyers keeping their clients out of prison -- that, after all,
is their job, even if the clients are guilty. The point is that Marley
was very well connected with the power elite. McCain & Marley,
check the material available about the mafia connection. Bolles
was killed when a bomb was detonated beneath his car. He lived
long enough to gasp, "They finally got me. The Mafia. Emprise.
Sen. McCain has been seen in the company of the principals of
Emprise, according to Sampley.

THE MOST IMPORTANT ELECTION EVER, OUR OWN DEMOCRACY DEPENDS ON IT !!

"The recent formation of the Congressional Israel Allies Caucus should. . . be noted as well as AIPAC's highlighting of the threat from Iran at its 2006 convention in Washington, an event that featured Vice President Dick Cheney as keynote speaker. More recently, Senator Hillary Clinton addressed an AIPAC gathering in New York City. Neither was shy about threatening Iran. AIPAC's formulation that the option of force 'must remain on the table' when dealing with Iran has been repeated like a mantra by numerous politicians and government officials, not too surprisingly as AIPAC writes the briefings and position papers that many Congressmen unfortunately rely on."

The American Israel Political Action Committee is the main political force urging - indeed, demanding - U.S. action. That's the AIPAC already under scrutiny for receiving classified information about Iran from Lawrence Franklin, former Defense Department subordinate of Douglas Feith.

Now, as Israeli calls for a U.S. attack on Iran become more shrill by the day, AIPAC recognizes that the American people profoundly distrust Vice President Cheney and the nest of neocon liars he has sheltered. The Bush-Cheney war machine has been pretty well exposed, and that must worry the warmongers within the group. Israeli Defense Force chief artillery officer Gen. Oded Tira has griped that "President Bush lacks the political power to attack Iran," adding that since "an American strike in Iran is essential for [Israel's] existence, we must help him pave the way by lobbying the Democratic Party.

Former CIA counterterrorism specialist Philip Giraldi, comparing the propaganda campaign against Iran to that which preceded the war on Iraq, has recently declared, "It is absolutely parallel."

"They're using the same dance steps-demonize the bad guys, the pretext of diplomacy, keep out of negotiations, use proxies. It is Iraq redux."

Former CIA counterterrorism specialist Philip Giraldi, comparing the propaganda campaign against Iran to that which preceded the war on Iraq, has recently declared, "It is absolutely parallel."

Unfortunately the Congress dominated by Democrats elected in a popular expression of antiwar sentiment has not taken a firm stance against an attack on Iran based on lies. Simply stated they are again controlled by a foreign lobby and their special interest MONEY.

The American voter has to break the grip of all lobbies on congress by voting such incumbents out of office. Demand restriction of lobbies.

Uri Lubrani, senior advisor to "Defense" Minister Amir Peretz, tells the Jewish Agency's Board of Governors that the U.S. "does not understand the threat and has not done enough," and therefore "must be shaken awake."

Tira urges the Lobby ((AIPAC)to turn to "potential presidential candidates. . . so that they support immediate action against Iran.

Many Americans would find such statements deeply offensive in their arrogance and condescension. President Bush has indeed been weakened by the "Iraq failure" Tira acknowledges, arising from a war that the Lobby demanded with enormous enthusiasm.

So now, the Israeli war advocates avert, the U.S. president needs to be helped to do the right thing and attack Iran by foreign lobbyists who will use their power to force the fools in the Democratic Party, especially presidential candidates.

Hillary Clinton has appeared at their convention, and has accepted their blood money for her campaign. She is being sucked in again, the same as Iraq. Her ticket to the presidency is the support of AIPAC, and their mainstream media.

John McCain, has come from the shadows to lead the Republican party on this bipartisan WAR machine rhetoric, also loves AIPAC & Israel. They call him their "Butt-Boy", he loves them so much he will sniff their asses.

Selecting AIPAC's #1 butt boy or girl is no easy task. One could easily throw a dart at a group picture of congress and find a perfectly suitable candidate. The ethical and moral collapse of our congress in all matters concerning Israel is now complete. Our foreign policy has been surrendered to Israel and their treasonous minions in this county, AIPAC.

"Knowing that to cross the Lobby is perilous, Congressmen from both parties squirm and become uneasy when pressured by AIPAC to 'protect Israel,' even if it means yet another un-winnable war for the United States. The neocons know full well that if a war with Iran were to be started either inadvertently or by design, few within America's political system would be brave enough to stand up in opposition."

AMERICA IS AWAKENED,
WE SUPPORT OBAMA.

A candidate, not accepting their rhetoric or money. We say and ask him to stand with us.

No thanks this time, AIPAC. You're just not credible. Can't do it for you. My constituents aren't into more war, and they think this whole Iran thing's a lot of hype. I can't support nuking Iran, and frankly, I don't see how you can either. I don't think you speak for all or even most American Jews, and you can't scare me this time by accusations of anti-Semitism.

I can't have an attack on Iran my conscience, sorry. I'd rather be defeated in the next election. Keep your money; I just can't do what you ask.

Will the Congress targeted by the Lobby be able to say that? If it doesn't, all the belated, posturing moves to limit Bush's power, withdraw troops and end the imperialist war in Iraq will mean nothing. An attack on Iran will unleash the gates of hell.

The fascistic proclivities of the administration will blossom immediately. The legal basis has been laid for the repression of the dissent an Iran attack will naturally inspire. Prison camps, suspension of habeas corpus. The proponents of the war are comfortable with these things, and the waters have already been tested.

In attacking the USS Liberty, Israel committed acts of murder against American servicemen and an act of war against the United States.

That fearing conflict with Israel, the White House deliberately prevented the U.S. Navy from coming to the defense of USS Liberty.

The Captain and surviving crew members were later threatened with court-martial, imprisonment or worse if they exposed the truth; and were abandoned by their own government.

That due to the influence of Israels powerful supporters in the United States, the White House deliberately covered up the facts of this attack from the American people.

That a danger to our national security exists whenever our elected officials are willing to subordinate American interests to those of any foreign nation, and specifically are unwilling to challenge Israels interests when they conflict with American interests.

On the 30th anniversary of Israels destruction of the liberty, Admiral Moorer said that Israel attacked the Liberty because Israel knew that the intelligence ship could intercept Israel plans to seize the Golan Heights from Syria, an act of Israeli aggression to which the US government was opposed. Admiral Moorer said, I believe Moshe Dayan concluded that he could prevent Washington from becoming aware of what Israel was up to by destroying the primary source of acquiring that information--the US Liberty.

Moorer reports that after a 25 minute air attack that pounded the Liberty with bombs, rockets, napalm and machine gun fire ... three Israeli torpedo boats closed in for the kill ... the torpedo boats machine guns also were turned on life rafts that were deployed into the Mediterranean as well as those few on deck that had escaped damage.

Admiral Moorer says, What is so chilling and cold-blooded, of course, is that they [Israel] could kill as many Americans as they did in confidence that Washington would cooperate in quelling any public outcry. The US invasion of Iraq and the looming US attack on Iran are proof that Israel has even more power over the White House today.

Israel's Gaza holocaust rhetoric should prompt the international community to take   Punitive measures against Israel including sanctions Measures to protect Palestinians against Israeli attack

No action

Results

Punitive measures against Israel including sanctions (70%)

Measures to protect Palestinians against Israeli attack (19%)

No action (11%)

JEWISH ORGANIZED CRIME

There have been many new developments in Jewish organized crime during the past few years, and although the mass media have carefully avoided talking about these developments, never using the word "Jew" and referring only to "Russian" organized crime when they do occasionally mention the subject, a new book was published just a few weeks ago by Little, Brown and Company, which provides an up-to-date and reasonably good introduction to the topic of Jewish organized crime.

Both in Russia and in the United States, members of the Jewish mobs machine-gun and bomb each other today even more readily than the members of the Italian gangs used to shoot it out in Chicago back in the 1930s. And although we adopt the standard media ploy of referring to the gangsters as "Russians," we really cannot help revealing that nearly all of them are Jews.

There is reluctance of the FBI and local and state police to crack down on the so-called "Russian Mafia" or even to investigate it,

State and Federal law enforcement agencies were loath to go after Russian mobsters, instead devoting their energies to bagging Italian wise guys .... And because the Russian mob was mostly Jewish, it was a political hot potato, especially in the New York area.

"Respectable" Jewish organizations, such as the Anti-Defamation League of B'nai B'rith, pressured the police agencies to take it easy on their kinsmen in the Jewish crime gangs, claiming that any publicity associated with investigations or arrests would "foster anti-Semitism" and lead the Gentile public to protest against the continued influx of Jewish gangsters into the United States from the Soviet Union as "refugees." Even after the collapse of the Soviet Union in 1991.

Jewish organizations continued to lobby the Justice Department to downplay the threat posed by the Russian mob. 'The Russian Mafia has the lowest priority on the criminal pecking order, it hasn't been too difficult lobbying Clinton & McCain to be nice to Jewish gangsters, since they have been the source of so much of their campaign money.

Sheltering the flood of Jewish thugs, extortionists, murderers, drug dealers, White slavers, and racketeers pouring in from Russia. The Jewish religious establishment in America did everything it could to facilitate the influx. That's a noteworthy point because the Jewish gangsters are portrayed by apologists for the Jews as being barely Jewish, Jews with no real consciousness of being Jewish, while the Jewish religious establishment is portrayed as being a pious bunch of rabbis, especially the Orthodox Jewish establishment. Actually it was in the Orthodox establishment that the gangsters formed their most useful connections.

So, if these Jewish mobsters get invited to Democratic Party fundraisers and serve as advisers to Republican reelection committees and are in tight with the Orthodox Jewish religious establishment, and if the FBI thinks they're not really as important as the Italian gangsters, maybe we shouldn't worry about them either. Maybe they're really not such bad guys. Maybe they're just nice, Jewish boys who sometimes step over the line and break the law.

A member of the John Gotti gang in New York was recorded with a wiretap warning an acquaintance:

We Italians will kill you. But the Russians are crazy -- they'll kill your whole family.

This view also is shared by policemen, politicians, business men, journalist, judges, and lawyers who have had to deal with the Jews.

The Russians are ruthless and crazy. It's a bad combination. They'll shoot you just to see if their gun works.

One leading Jewish gangster in the United States, Monya Elson, was a hit man, a contract killer, before he became a gang boss. He began by murdering Ukrainians in Kishinev, his home town. Then he went to Moscow and murdered Russians. Then he came to America and began murdering Americans. He boasts that he has more than 100 confirmed kills. And it's not just that the Jews are more ruthless, vicious, and bloodthirsty than the members of the Italian Mafia. They are smarter, better organized, better protected politically, and much greedier: while the Mafia is stealing a million dollars, the Jews are stealing a billion. Finally, there are many more Jewish gangsters in America than Italian Mafia members.

Jews are continuing to pour into the country from Russia. The current flood began nearly 30 years ago, when corrupt politicians in the Congress, working with mainstream Jewish organizations and the Jewish media, enacted legislation that opened a sewer line from the Soviet-Jewish underworld to America.

The FBI has essentially put the Italian Mafia out of business in the United States during the past decade, but it won't put the Jewish Mafia out of business, and the reason is that the Jews have vastly more money at their disposal for corrupting the system than the Italians ever did, and America has become as corruptible as Russia.

The Jewish Mafia does not operate in a vacuum. It operates within the Jewish community as a whole. It operates with the support of the Jewish establishment, from the Anti-Defamation League of B'nai B'rith to Hollywood and the New York Times. It also operates with the support of the Christian establishment, from Billy Graham up to the Pope. These support groups won't put up a fuss if the FBI arrests a Jewish contract killer or a Jewish extortionist or two now and then, but any realistic effort to stamp out the whole cedillas will have all of the support groups screaming bloody murder. To use other words, what we must deal with is not a criminal problem but a Jewish problem. The problem will be solved only after this fact is generally understood. Meanwhile, the American sheep had better resign themselves to a good fleecing. Of course that has been happening for the last 15-20 years.

The real national mission is to clear out all of the centers of organized crime. Olmert, who waged a well-publicized war against another organized crime apparatus at the beginning of his career, should know this. The crime apparatus he now faces is strong, violent and immeasurably more dangerous than the Siboni brothers from Mevasseret Yerushalayim, whom he confronted precisely 30 years ago. At that time, he faced off against those who were intimidating a small town. Now he is facing those who are holding an entire state hostage. The United States is in the same situation, the government is held hostage. The greed took over and is destroying the nation.

Prepare for ruff times ahead. Complete take over. Or fight with the revolution. The decision will be up to you, the citizens of this Country we all love.

The End or Beginning??

Biggest deceptions: 1. Fascism==Democracy!
    2. Christianity==Rapture!
    3. That our young people are naive, and do
    not recognize the problems facing them.
That they will not revolt against such anarchy.

Do you agree that the U.S. should delay its troop withdrawal from Iraq as recommended by General Petraeus?

Yes (24.82%)

No (75.18%)

Total Voters: 1983

Will the new spy scandal affect U.S.-Israeli ties?
The U.S. arrested an American on charges of spying for Israel, in a case linked to the Pollard spy scandal that rocked U.S.-Israeli relations. NO The Media and officials are already covering it up.

"The U.S. knows no accountability!"
Bush will not be held accountable for his actions and even if he were, it would not stop his self-righteousness.

60 YEARS OF ILLEGAL OCCUPATION, SUPPORTED BY USA OFFICIALS, BUT NOT THE AMERICAN PEOPLE.

SILENCE, OR BE SILENCED IS THE MOTTO OF THE GROUP.

Just as Israel inaugurated its misbegotten birth with genocidal ethnic cleansing sixty years ago, the evil brat of Zionism is marking its 60th anniversary with yet another spate of bloodletting.

On Sunday, 27 April, the Israeli "Defense" Forces (a more appropriate appellation would be the Jewish Wehrmacht) murdered a mother and her four children in Beit Hanoun, a northern Gaza suburb.

The mother and her kids reportedly were having breakfast when an artillery shell fired from an Israeli Merkava battle-tank hit their home, killing them instantly and mutilating their bodies.

The graphic, blood-splattered images of the mutilated children and their mother raised no eyebrows among Israeli leaders and the Zionist-Jewish public opinion. After all, these Nazi-minded and Nazi-hearted Zionists have been doing this for more than sixty years.

And the world seems to be coming to terms with these crimes as a fact of life. This is at least how Israel views world reactions to its crimes against the peoples of the Middle East.

Anyone familiar with the Zionist way of thinking would tell you that whenever a pornographic carnage is committed by the Israeli occupation army, Israeli leaders don't indulge in soul-searching over the barbarian behavior they engage in. Instead, they just activate their hasbara machine in order to control the resulting public relations damage and help exonerate Israel of any wrong doing before the eyes of the world.

Thus, these evil child killers have told us that their victims were killed not by Israeli artillery shells, but rather by Palestinian explosives! Well, didn't these wicked liars claim that Muhammed Durra was killed by Palestinian snipers in order to tarnish Israel's image?

This is of course not the first time the Israeli army murders an entire family in order to inflict "shock and awe" on a people as bent on living and surviving as Israel is bent on killing and murdering.

Israel's history, after all, has been an uninterrupted concatenation of massacres and war crimes. In fact, one would exaggerate very little by saying that Israel itself is a crime against humanity, and for that matter a continuing crime against humanity.

The latest carnage in Gaza didn't occur in isolation. The entire Gaza Strip has been languishing under a harsh blockade that has much in common with the Nazi blockade of the Warsaw Ghetto in Poland in 1943.

This is a truth that many people in Europe and North America can't bring themselves to accept, at least openly, because it is not politically correct to do so. Well, does the West need to see a full-fledged holocaust in Palestine in order to cast the holocaust guilt off its shoulders? Must Palestinian children be slaughtered every morning and every evening in order to finally bring about the long-awaited recuperation of Europe from the holocaust complex?

As a result of barring the estimated 1.5 million Gaza inhabitants from accessing food, work, medicine and fuel, the vast bulk of the population has been forced into abject poverty and virtual starvation.

Ill people who can't find the needed medicine and required medical care in local health facilities, are left to succumb to their illnesses.

It is believed that more than 200 innocent Gazan patients have so far died as a direct result of the callous Nazi-like siege.

This happens as Israeli officials appearing on western TV screens keep assuring the mostly nonchalant or morally-apathetic western audiences that under no circumstances would Israel allow a "humanitarian crisis" to develop in Gaza. Well, what, apart from lies, do we expect from Zionism, a Godless, satanic ideology based on murder, theft and mendacity?

What do we expect from a state that sends its crack soldiers to raid and terrorize orphanages and boarding schools in Hebron in the dead of night?

What do we expect from a state that confiscates donated food for orphaned children whose parents had been murdered by the Israeli army.a state that orders its soldiers to raid inventory warehouses and steal shoes, clothes, even underwear, of orphaned children under ten years of age?

What do we expect from a state whose soldiers murder 12-year-old school kids, and then verify the kill by emptying 20 more bullets into the small victim's body to make sure that the dead or dying little girl or boy doesn't pose a threat to the security and safety of the heroic soldier?

What do we expect from a state whose army bulldozers crush peace activists to death and then tells the world that " the bulldozer driver acted in accordance with outstanding instructions and did nothing wrong."

Obviously, a sate as such is a Nazi state par excellence.

Well, I know that Israel has produced good scientists and built good hospitals and made impressive achievements in science, technology and other fields.

But this doesn't mean much in moral terms. Nazi Germany, too, produced many good scientists, built many good hospitals and made impressive achievements in science and technology.

Besides, what is the point of inventing advanced electronic devices and then using the technology in murdering and maiming sleeping children and women and other innocent civilians?

Indeed, what is the point of building a prosperous state on a foundation of oppression, mass murder and ethnic cleansing?

Israel may appear modern, vigorous and democratic to much of the outside world. But for us, the Palestinians, Israel is and will always be a murderer, a thief and a liar.

Israel stole our country away from us, ethnically cleansed our people, destroyed our homes, bulldozed our towns and villages, poisoned our water wells lest we return, and then expelled the bulk of our people to the four corners of the globe.these are the very people Israeli leaders and spokespersons now shamelessly call "terrorists."

Yes, Israel is militarily and economically powerful; it has a huge stockpile of nuclear weapons, and pro-Israeli pressure groups control the American government as well as much of the media and show business in the United States.

So what?

Evil states, like evil people, do not last forever.

The Hidden Architecture of U.S. Militarism:

Militarism as "advocacy of an ever-stronger military as a primary goal of society, even at the cost of other social priorities and liberties." And it relates militarism to chauvinism, fascism, and national socialism. As uncomfortable as it may be for many, this chilling definition accurately describes the historical trajectory and current reality of U.S. national security policy. The threatened first use of nuclear weapons remains at the heart of that policy, and at the core of StratCom's mission.

This architecture is "hidden in plain sight." All of the information presented here is available from open sources. None of it is classified, yet it is hidden from public view, barely mentioned in the mainstream media, and the U.S. arms control establishment chooses largely to ignore it because of the complexities it introduces into the short-term, "pragmatic" mindset prevalent in Washington, DC.

As distinct from other peoples, most Americans do not recognize -- or do not want to recognize -- that the United States dominates the world through its military power. Due to government secrecy, our citizens are often ignorant of the fact that our garrisons encircle the planet. This vast network of American bases on every continent except Antarctica actually constitutes a new form of empire -- an empire of bases with its own geography not likely to be taught in any high school geography class. Without grasping the dimensions of this globe-girdling Baseworld, one can't begin to understand the size and nature of our imperial aspirations or the degree to which a new kind of militarism is undermining our constitutional order.

Our military deploys well over half a million soldiers, spies, technicians, teachers, dependents, and civilian contractors in other nations. To dominate the oceans and seas of the world, we are creating some thirteen naval task forces built around aircraft carriers whose names sum up our martial heritage. . . . We operate numerous secret bases outside our territory to monitor what the people of the world, including our own citizens, are saying, faxing, or e-mailing to one another."

Johnson also explains how the U.S. military economy not only directly profits private corporations and their sub-contractors, by developing and producing weapons for the armed forces and servicing the needs of military personnel, but also in more indirect and unexpected ways.

"On the eve of our second war on Iraq, for example, while the Defense Department was ordering up an extra ration of cruise missiles and depleted-uranium armor-piercing tank shells, it also acquired 273,000 bottles of Native Tan sunblock, almost triple its 1999 order and undoubtedly a boon to the supplier,...and its subcontractor, Sun Fun Products of Daytona Beach, Florida."

Noting that "official records on these subjects are misleading," Johnson in 2004 estimated that the Pentagon maintains more than 700 overseas bases in about 130 countries, with an additional 6,000 bases in the United States and its territories. He concludes:

"These numbers, although staggeringly large, do not begin to cover all the actual bases we occupy globally.... If there were an honest count, the actual size of our military empire would probably top 1,000 different bases in other people's countries, but no one -- possibly not even the Pentagon -- knows the exact number for sure, although it has been distinctly on the rise in recent years.

The United States military dominates the globe through its operation of 10 Unified Combatant Commands. Composed of forces from two or more armed services, the Unified Commands are headed by four-star generals and admirals who operate under the direct authority of the Secretary of Defense, accountable only to the President. Six of the Commands are responsible for designated regions of the world, and the four others for various operations. It is a mind-numbing exercise just to list them all, but in order to comprehend the breadth and depth of U.S. militarism, it is absolutely essential to be aware of their existence.

In a 2006 review of this study and two other surveys of U.S. military interventions, journalist Gar Smith found that "in our country's 230 years of existence, there have been only 31 years in which U.S. troops were not actively engaged in significant armed adventures on foreign shores." He concluded:

"The arithmetic is daunting. Over the long course of U.S. history, fewer than 14% of America's days have been marked by peace. The defining characteristic of our nation's foreign policy for 86% of our existence would appear to be a bellicose penchant for military intervention.

As of 2006, there were 192 member states in the United Nations. Incredibly enough, over the past two centuries, the United State has attacked, invaded, policed, overthrown or occupied 62 of them."

"[E]mpire has a much longer history than just the Bush administration, and I would be the first to argue... that Bill Clinton was a better imperialist than George Bush because he cleverly disguised what we were doing under various rubrics that he invented.... For example, Clinton argued that our attack on Serbia in 1999 was humanitarian intervention. In other cases, he disguised our imperialism as part of a newly discovered inevitable process called 'globalization'."

Another not so hidden part of the architecture of U.S. militarism is the incredible amount of money the U.S. has spent - and is spending - on its military enterprise.

The Center for Strategic and Budgetary Assessments estimates that the United States currently spends approximately $54 billion annually on all nuclear-related programs and activities including offensive and defensive capabilities, Department of Defense and Department of Energy activities, strategic and theater forces, as well as associated command, control and communications capabilities. That is more than the entire military budget of nearly every individual country in the world. In 2006, only China ($121.9 B), Russia ($70.B), the United Kingdom ($55.4B), and France ($54.B) spent $54 billion or more in total on their militaries.

What else could $54 billion a year be used for? According to the 1998 United Nations Development Program report, the additional cost of achieving and maintaining universal access to basic education for all, basic health care for all, reproductive health care for all women, adequate food for all, and clean water and safe sewers for all would amount to roughly $40 billion a year.

On February 4, the Bush administration released its budget request for Fiscal Year 2009, which begins Oct. 1, 2008. For FY 2009, the White House is seeking $711 Billion for the military - $541 for the Pentagon and the nuclear weapons-related activities of the DOE, and according to Defense Secretary Robert Gates, at least $170 Billion for ongoing military operations in Iraq and Afghanistan.

In a chapter entitled, "Redefining Security in Human Terms," we grappled with the problem of relating abolition of nuclear weapons to demilitarization and a new concept of security. Our conclusion is that a paradigm shift is called for; a fundamental reconceptualization of security, from which a new system can emerge, from the bottom up. There are recommendations:

The concept of security should be reframed at every level of society and government, with a premium on universal human and ecological security, a return to multilateralism, and a commitment to cooperative, nonviolent means of conflict resolution.

Nuclear disarmament should serve as the leading edge of a global trend towards demilitarization and redirection of military expenditures to meet human and environmental needs. The United States government has a special responsibility to take leadership in this massive undertaking.

The United States government, however, will not take leadership in this massive undertaking without a massive nonviolent demand from below. And we Americans can't create that demand alone. We, the ordinary people of the world, must recognize that we are all in this together!

AMERICANS WILL STAY VIGILANT.

This government now faces revolution from the American people, there has never been a time that the American people were so angry due to none of the official representatives actually represent the PEOPLE, they are there, bought and paid for by special interest, represent corruption, foreign lobbies, organized crime, and huge corporations foreign & domestic. (HOW ABOUT US THE VOTERS) AIPAC and affiliates, have influenced our government, to the point of control. We face a large amount of people with duel citizenship, able to vote here and else where, even by absentee ballots. Such duel citizens can run for office. Such should be illegal, it is not in the interest of America or American people.

Torture, human rights violation, false intelligence, no bid contracts, and duel citizenship voting' are all UNJUST to the American People. Fight for change.

Do not "underestimate" the "anger," "frustration," and "determination," of your citizens who demand "justice and fairness."

"Injustice anywhere is injustice everywhere".

Fair taxation, 68% of corporations paying no tax at all are not considered "FAIR" by anyone we know.

We will fight for change, we support Obama.

While foreign contributions to presidential campaigns are illegal and Americans are limited to $2,300 per election, some candidates skirt the law by accepting millions of dollars from foreigners and favor-seeking U.S. citizens through some foundation.

We the American citizens have raised the funds for Obama, none has come from the special interest groups.

America and the American people are Obama's special interest group.

ETHICS, INTEGRITY, MORALITY, TRUTH, AND INTELLIGENCE, THAT MAKES THE DIFFERENCE!!

Regarding religion. I feel the moral values of real justice;and hate injustice in the World. BUT I can not follow any of the organized religious rhetoric, and doctrine that we witness. Self rightous -- War mongering, and profiteers. The real hypocracy.

I know the feeling of doubt. I think Obama is our only chance, if we have one at all. We need to start some where. At least he does not accept money from the special interest. We the people raised his funds, quite well in fact. It will take all of us to stay on top of it, and make our voices are heard. Watch groups next. (AND) We need to make sure that AIPAC and other lobbies are kept out of the white house & the halls of congress.

On Thursday, Speaker Nancy Pelosi will force the House to approve $163 billion more of our tax dollars for the occupation of Iraq - nearly $100 billion for 2008 plus nearly $70 billion more for 2009.

We are outraged. This Democratic Congress was elected to end the occupation, not fund it forever.

Is your retirement at risk because of waste, fraud and corruption in Iraq? The largest contractor in Iraq is KBR, formerly a Halliburton subsidiary. The same Halliburton that Dick Cheney ran until he decided to campaign for Vice President. How bad is it? No bid contracts, offshore tax havens, massive fraud, and even claims of rape.

Despite these well known problems with KBR, major retirement and pension funds continue to invest in the company. Public employee retirement systems in states including California, New York, Ohio and Texas have millions of dollars invested in a company with a horrendous track record.

On the eve of Congress passing the largest war funding bill yet, $178 billion, Iraqi mothers struggling to survive are being denied in favor of endless war. This Mother's Day, as we honor the women who gave us life, let's help give new hope to women whose lives have been shattered by the US occupation.

Peace 4 All, and an end to all illegal occupations.

(NEED FOR FOREIGN
POLICY CHANGES)

Israeli Minister: Iran Could Go Nuclear This Year Just more false and misleading intelligence, pushing fear, and another Iraq type cluster "screw-up".

Iran will likely have the means to produce nuclear weapons before the end of this year, warns Israeli Transportation Minister Shaul Mofaz.

A recent Israeli Military Intelligence assessment estimated that Iran would not be able to go nuclear until 2010. But Mofaz, a former defense minister and Israeli Defense Force chief of General Staff, said Iran could have the know-how to build nuclear arms within months. (Bull Crap)

In a speech at Yale University on the eve of Holocaust Remembrance Day, Mofaz said the diplomatic channel was the preferred way to stop Iran's nuclear program, but added that any means of ensuring that Iran does not acquire nuclear weapons are valid, according to the Jerusalem Post.

"Israel will not tolerate a nuclear Iran, and I'd like to believe that the rest of the world will not allow it to happen," Mofaz said. "All is fair in the efforts to make sure it doesn't happen." Then why should the Israeli regime have nuclear weapons. That has been the danger for the Middle East the past few years.

He also declared that the "Iranian regime is the number one threat to mankind in the 21st century. It is a multi-dimensional, multi-armed threat, which increases every day, every hour."

Photos taken during a recent visit by Iranian President Mahmoud Ahmadinejad to Natanz, where Iran is building centrifuges to enrich uranium, were released to the world press by Iran. They clearly show the progress Iran has made on installing the newer IR-2 model centrifuge, which appears ready for testing, according to HSToday, a Web site focusing on homeland security.

Mofaz was in the U.S. with an Israeli delegation holding meetings with American officials, including Secretary of State Condoleezza Rice.

Israeli Policy Makes a Two-State Solution Less Likely Summary of CNI Foundation "Public Hearing

Two Israeli peace activists told an audience in Washington, DC, that as long as current Israeli policies continue, a real two-state solution to the Israeli-Palestinian conflict is increasingly unlikely and perhaps impossible. The speakers were the Rev. Dr. Naim Ateek, founder and director of the Sabeel Ecumenical Liberation Theology Center in Jerusalem, and Jeff Halper, founder and coordinator of the Israeli Committee Against House Demolitions (ICAHD). Halper and Ateek spoke at the National Press Club, at the CNI Foundation's "public hearing" to bring a much-needed debate about U.S. Middle East policy to Washington, DC.

A streaming video of the event can be seen online at the following website: http://www.archive.org/details/Is_the_Two-State_Solution_Still_Possible

Halper stated that his background as an anthropologist taught him to see things "from the ground up" and to "go where the field takes him," even if it means he has to ocasionally admit that he is wrong. As a peace activist, Halper said he believes that while a "two-state solution" to the Israeli-Palestinian conflict is an article of faith among Israelis, Palestinians, and virtually every other party involved or interested in the conflict, activists should admit that such an outcome is no longer possible because of Israel's policy of apartheid in the territories. He said that this position has made him a pariah among American groups, such as Americans for Peace Now and the Foundation for Middle East Peace, who refuse to host him for public talks.

In short, Halper said that the two-state solution is a "political program based on wishful thinking." He said he defines the word "apartheid" the same way as Jimmy Carter does in his book "Palestine Peace Not Apartheid": a separation of populations in which one people structurally and conceptually dominates the other permanently. One difference between Israeli apartheid and that of South Africa, Halper notes, is that Israel "feels like it can finesse a bantustan [for the Palestinians] in a way that South Africa could not."

As evidence he pointed to what he calls Israel's "matrix of control" in the occupied territories. The population of the Jewish-only settlements has more than doubled since Yasser Arafat's PLO recognized Israel, and thus endorsed the two-state solution, in 1988. The wall, the military checkpoints, and Israeli "bypass roads" criss-cross the West Bank and allow settlers easy travel, while carving up the territory and preventing Palestinian freedom of movement. Halper hinted at an alternative solution to the two-state model, which he calls a "two-stage" solution, based on an economic federation of Israel/Palestine and neighboring states.

Rev. Ateek cited scripture's command to "do justice and love mercy" as a reason why he once advocated for one state in Palestine, where, he said, "Jews, Muslims, and Christians can live together democratically." Later, he said he came to see that a one-state solution "may not be fair for a Jewish state," but that "a 'Jewish state' cannot be democratic." As a Palestinian Christian, he argued that, in the same way, an Islamic state in Palestine would not be democratic for the Christian minority. A one-state solution to the conflict would represent "justice without mercy."

As long as the final outcome is based on prior UN Security Council resolutions and international law, Ateek said that he would support a two-state solution. Specifically, he said that any solution must address the current disconnect between nationality and citizenship in the conflict. For example, he argued that Palestinians who live in Israel with Israeli citizenship, like himself, are not considered part of Israeli society, just as Israeli settlers living in the West Bank do not consider themselves Palestinian. He stated that he would tell the Israeli settlers, under any future agreement, "You are welcome to become Palestinians," but that until then, they are living illegally on Palestinian land. Any arrangement that takes justice and mercy as its basis must "protect the sovereignty of both states," which includes keeping "Palestinians secure from encroachment from their more powerful neighbor."

The event was sponsored by the Council for the National Interest Foundation and the Washington Interfaith Alliance for Middle East Peace. The moderator was Dr. Mark Braverman, board member of the Washington Interfaith Alliance on Middle East Peace and board member of Partners for Peace.

As we approach the 2008 elections, two paths lie before us. One leads to greater reliance on imported fuels, increased militarization of our foreign fuel dependency and prolonged struggle with other powers for control over the world's remaining supplies of fossil fuels. The other leads toward diminished reliance on petroleum as a main source of our fuel, the rapid development of energy alternatives, a reduced U.S. military profile abroad and cooperation with China in the development of innovative energy options. Rarely has a policy choice been as stark or as momentous for the future of our country.

(SEEMS FUNNY TO ME THAT OUR NAVY FAMILY HAS FORGOTTEN THIS HISTORY)

The 40th anniversary of the 1967 Middle East War brought back bad memories not just for Arabs, but also for many Americans.

On 8 June 1967, fighter planes and torpedo boats attacked the USS Liberty off the coast of Egypt. The surprise attack, which lasted about 40 minutes, killed 34 American servicemen, and wounded at least 173.

Surprisingly, the attack came from the U.S.'s closest ally, Israel. It was the second-deadliest ambush against a U.S. warship since the end of World War II, surpassed only by the Iraqi Exocet missile attack on the USS Stark on May 17th, 1987, and marked the single greatest loss of life by the U.S. intelligence community.

Several U.S. and Israeli investigations, and the declassification of thousands of pieces of information, didn't reveal the truth. Liberty survivors and several top U.S. officials believe (KNOW) that the truth was covered up. They stress that the USS Liberty was more than twice as large as the El Quseir, and was clearly designated with Latin rather than Arabic letters and numbers.

Gary Brummett, a 21-year-old third class petty officer who was serving on board the USS Liberty, also believes that the attack was a war crime and that American and Israeli authorities were and are still covering up the incident. "I have more trouble with it today than when it happened because I know more of the facts about what was going on," he told BBC. "There's been an egregious wrong done here, there have been an extreme number of lies told to the American people and the American people do not know the truth about what happened."

Skeptics believe that the attack was premeditated and that the truth has been covered up. Such beliefs were strengthened by a 2003 independent commission of inquiry which reported that the attack on the Liberty "remains the only serious naval incident that has never been thoroughly investigated by Congress".

There are multiple theories regarding the real reason behind the deadly attack; the gravest incident in the history of U.S.-Israeli relations.

One of the most powerful assertions of a cover-up also came from retired U.S. Navy lawyer Capt Ward Boston, counsel to the Navy Court of Inquiry into the incident conducted just days after the attack. Capt. Boston asserts that the court's original findings, which he signed, were changed afterwards by government lawyers. He also says that the president of the court, Rear Adm Isaac Kidd, told him he was ordered by U.S. President Lyndon Johnson and Defense Secretary Robert McNamara to conclude the attack was a case of mistaken identity.

The men who served America onboard the Liberty have been forced to carry the truth of this war crime against the US and its citizens to their graves due to the power of Israeli lobbyists and politicians. These men who gave their lives deserved to have their story told, not hidden behind secrecy and cover ups. Please do these men some justice by researching the facts by yourself. One of Americas most highly decorated Admirals commissioned his own enquiry into this incident and found that Israel had indeed deliberately targeted the liberty in a "False flag" black operation.

1963   ASSASSINATION. JFK

1967   ATTACK ON USS LIBERTY

4/68 ASSASSINATION MLK

6/68 ASSASSINATION RFK

CHECK OUT MEYER LANSKI HISTORY, WHO HE WAS.

HOW ABOUT NEW ORLEAN'S GARRISON AND WITNESSES.

60 YEARS OF GENOCIDE OF PALESTINE.

911 QUESTIONS WILL NEVER BE ANSWERED.

FALSE INTELLIGENCE FROM MOSSAD ON IRAQ.

MORE FALSE INFORMATION AND PRE-EMPTIVE ATTACK PLAN FOR IRAN.

CONNECT THE DOTS FOLKS.....

WHAT HAVE WE BEEN TOLD ABOUT PERMANENT BASES?

US army is completing the building of military facilities and runways for permanent bases 03 Jun 2008 A proposed Iraqi-American security agreement will include permanent American bases in the country, and the right for the United States to strike, from within Iraqi territory, any country it considers a threat to its national security, Gulf News has learned. Senior Iraqi military sources have told Gulf News that the long-term controversial agreement is likely to include three major items:

- Iraqi security institutions such as Defense, Interior and National Security ministries, as well as armament contracts, will be under US supervision for ten years

- Agreement is also likely to give US forces permanent military bases in Iraq

- US is granted the right to move against any country considered to be a threat against world stability or acting against Iraqi or American interests.

HOW ABOUT REPORTING ON THE TOTAL HISTORY

OF THOSE TIMES UP TO NOW & WHY NOT ?

SEPERATION OF CHURCH & STATE:

The Separation of Church and State principle is a part of our historical, legal and political / social heritage and preserves and protects our religious liberty. Our page is devoted to exploring the nature and purpose of this principle in an effort to educate the public. We also intend this page to provide a resource to anyone involved in the on-going Church and State debate.

The purpose is to create a response to the religious right's anti-separationist / accomodationist / non-preferentialist views.

We want to go in depth into the legal, historical and political / social evidence that exists to support separation of church and state. We do not plan to stop there, but will dig deeper into the meaning, purpose and use of the principle of separation of church and state. the church / state debate is a timely issue which merits an on-going monitoring of current events. We want to continue to post new information about court battles, proposed amendments, state action and church / state events.

The Constitutional Principle:

Separation of Church and State

Religious Liberty: Our Heritage from the Founding Fathers

Presently, and for the past several years, there are foreign & religious lobbies that interfere, and influence our officials, attempt to change our laws, and leads to an attempt to discredit our

Christian faith and our rights to worship as we please, which was granted by OUR constitution.

We have lobbies not registered as foreign, openly operating and spreading their propaganda.

Organized groups do attempt to directly affect legislation. One of these, the American-Israel Public Affairs Committee (AIPAC) is a registered lobby.

U.S. Middle East policy is further shaped by Jewish voting behavior and American public opinion. These indirect means of influence are the informal lobby which spreads their propaganda though media, academia, and promoting the myth of being God's chosen people. (denying the New Testament). The Israeli lobby can then be defined as those formal and informal actors that directly and indirectly influence American policy to support Israel.

Regardless of ones faith & beliefs, none should be influencing our laws, constitution or elected officials in government by the people, it is not a government for a select few.

The first pro-Israel PAC was formed in 1978, but there was little activity until 1982 when thirty-three pro-Israel PACs contributed $1.87 million to congressional candidates. According to the Center for Responsive Politics, pro-Israel interests have contributed $58 million in individual, PAC, and soft money contributions to national-level candidates and national party committees. The PACs' contributions became increasingly focused in 1984 and, apparently, they had a high degree of success in choosing winning candidates. Of course for their interest, not the American people. Such has lead to the government for SALE of the last two administrations. CHECK out all contributions, and to whom. (We need change, we need Obama, and we need to renew American vision & values.)

In return for these efforts, look at the foreign aid , military equipment, cluster bombs, missles, and even nukes. Then loans that will never be repaid. Foreign trade, and on and on. (redistricting). The organization that directly lobbies the U.S. government on behalf of the Israeli lobby is AIPAC. The lobby, originally called the American Zionist Committee for Public Affairs, was founded in

1951. Just 3 years after the stealing Palestinian lands, and forming the illegal State of Israel. The atrocities of such, with USA support, continue today. Right near the time that ZIONIST come up with the propaganda of rapture. Some people believing such to today, influencing Christian theologist to preach such false eschatology.

AIPAC has the luxury of being able to call its allies in Congress to pass along information, and then leaves much of the work of writing bills and gathering cosponsors to the legislative staffs. The lobbyists themselves are mostly Capitol Hill veterans who know how to operate the levers of power.

The Israeli lobby depends on the network it has developed to galvanize the Jewish community to take some form of political action. The network consists of at least seventy-five different organizations, which in one way or another support Israel. Most cannot legally engage in lobbing, but are represented on the Board of Directors of AIPAC, so they are able to provide input into the lobby's decision-making process. Equally important is the bureaucratic machinery of these organizations, which enables them to disseminate information to their members and facilitate a rapid response to legislative activity.

U.S. commitment to Israel — has been accepted as a national interest. The Israeli lobby is a powerful and dangerous influence that controls U.S. policy.

The Israeli lobby has won; that is, achieved its policy objective, 60 percent of the time. The most important variable was the president's position. When the president, such as Clinton & Bush, supports the lobby, it won 95 percent of the time. The Kennedy's did not support the lobby, they were of course Catholic, and history shows what happened.

We need change, but let's hope history does not repeat itself as the Clinton's have suggested.

LOOKS LIKE HILLARY'S PLAN TO PLANT SEEDS INTO THE MINDS OF "CRAZIES" WORKS WELL!!

FOX Contributor Liz Trotta jokingly wished for the assassination of Sen. Barack Obama.

I'm sure she was speaking for AIPAC as well. Haven't we seen enough assassinations by these people? It is time to close in on the real criminal element in our society. (Foreign lobby and their pundits)

From Fox she most likely will get promoted, but we can attempt to FORCE accountability, even though It will be fake.

Go to: AIPAC web page and check out the areas of influence. Goggle AIPAC and related sites for information on the violations by religious organization.

Protect OUR constitution; elect a president that will preserve our constitution. "OBAMA"

Quick Vote
1. Do you believe Presidential candidates are more committed to pandering to ethnic and other special interest groups than to this country's national interest?
Yes   96%   3083
No   4%   136
Total Votes: 3219

2. This is not a scientific poll

THANK YOU Dennis Kucinich for Introducing Articles of Impeachment!

"We've waited seven years to find one Member of Congress brave enough to stand up for our Constitution, for which generations of Americans have fought and died. We are thrilled and honored that Dennis Kucinich has chosen to be that one genuine patriot. We congratulate him on his historic leadership, and pledge to do everything in our power to persuade Congress to adopt all 35 Articles and put George W. Bush on trial before the Senate of the United States, exactly as the Founding Fathers wanted."

"Some might question why Congressman Kucinich has done this now. My question is why 434 other Congress Members have not done it before. Despite the uncountable and unspeakable crimes this administration has committed, George Bush and Dick Cheney remain in power and immune from prosecution. Congress must impeach Bush and Cheney now - before they further abuse their power by pardoning for all of their crimes."

Bush has had many accomplices, first and foremost Vice President Cheney. But our Founders created a single executive precisely so that we could hold that one person accountable for the actions of the Executive Branch. It is high time we did so, and millions of Americans will be urging their representatives to support the effort being led by Congressman Kucinich.

PEACE 4 ALL !

THE END !   PEACE 4 ALL

IT IS UP TO YOU AN ME.

Rep. Dennis Kucinich has introduced 35 articles of impeachment.

Ramsey Clark makes clear, the impeachment of George W. Bush is the most important task of the moment for the safety and security of the people of the United States, the Middle East and throughout the world. None of us can risk being plunged further into war.

Go to, and support: ImpeachBush.org

More than 1 million people have joined together in support of the impeachment movement.

The only morons that cannot be moved off their pompus asses to do the real business of & for the AMERICAN PEOPLE are the elected ignorant representatives in Congress and the Senate.

They can not disassociate themselves from the fact that they have rubber stamped each and every move made by Bush, and that they themselves have accepted funds from the same corporations, foreign lobbies, and no bid contractors that Bush/Cheney have.

I would suggest that a much deeper investigation into government corruption, and out side influences needs to be under-taken. BUT by who?

The list of those needing to be Impeached and prosecuted keeps growing.

Media, who controls it?

The Moral Church: If there is such a thing, who are they so heavily invested with?

CIA-FBI, Inter-Pol: What is their politics?

It all comes down to the citizens of this Great Country taking responcibility, becoming well informed. Take action, by voting responcibly, encouraging others to do the same. Demand watch groups, support such,by becoming involved. Think Tanks that are for us the American People, not foreign interest.Give back to your community by caring. 43% of eligible voters do not vote. Nor do they pay attention.

A revolution is well on the way, the people will unite,how-ever will it be constructive or destructive?

That my fellow Americans is up to us, you and me.

READ:
FINAL REPORT

This controversial new book written by a retired Police officer is a fact-loaded tableau exposing the inner-workings of our government in relation to foreign policy, nuclear armament, and political corruption.

He calls for a literal reprisal of our government though a return to " by the people" democracy.

Who, What, Where, When, Why & Wake-up !!

Order & Read : FINAL-REPORT.ID# 49149.

The easiest way to place an order is to go to the Author House Bookstore. You can also call our Book Order Hotline, at 888.280.7715.(Book ID# 49149) Also, orders can be accepted via email at bkorders@authorhouse.com.

OR: Web. site

http://www.authorhouse.com/bookstore/ItemDetail.aspx?bookid=49149

A second book: Titled DECEPTION; ID # 53223 will soon be available through the same outlets.

Both books also available at Barnes & Noble, and Amazon.com.

DO ALL YOU CAN, NOW.

Impeachment, a Constitutional duty, is the only way to prevent George W. Bush and his cabal from vastly enlarging the disastrous wars he has already inflicted on the world and the American people. The House of Representatives must quickly consider Bills of Impeachment long overdue, and the Senate must prepare to sit in judgment of President Bush, Vice President Cheney other officers who are implicated.

WILL THEY DO IT? ONLY BY BEING FORCED TO. NOT BY THE MORAL JUDGEMENT THEY SHOULD HAVE, THAT THEY MAY PROFESS TO HAVE, BUT AS YOU AND I KNOW, THAT

IS ONLY AT ELECTION TIME WITH MOST.

Obama is the candidate I trust presently.

ABOUT THE AUTHOR

I retired after serving several years in the criminal Justice fields of law enforcement, Public defenders office, Security, and prison correctional.

An interest developed for criminal justice after the assassination of President John F. Kennedy.

After serving in the US Army, I joined the police department, I'm high mileage, and been to a few fairs during my career, taking me to several areas around the Country.

The bay of pigs, Meyer Lanski, DA Garrison, Russian Jewish Mafia, The Gem Stone, Robert Kennedy, Martin L. King, Chain economy, fraudulent elections, corruption, Fascism, inciting racism, needless wars created, unfair trade agreements, outsourcing, no bid contracts, occupations, no over sight, immunity to security contractors, special interest lobbies, secrecy, outright lies, outing of CIA agents, destruction of evidence, torture, Black holes by white criminals, open borders, drug trade, and political parties, all these items seem to have dots that have connective lines. Several people interviewed, share the same frustrations.

Regardless of the outcome of investigations and hearings, there is enough evidence that the American people, need to force change.

ALL AMERICAN PEOPLE : African, Hispanic, Asian, Native, Poor and middle class Americans need to unite and demand CHANGE.

We voiced it to no avail 2006 elections, now we will demand it 2008 elections. Please help elect the candidate for change "Barack Obama".

YES, this is all about America, not the author.